THE CHURCH AND THE SACRAMENTS

THE CHURCH
AND THE SACRAMENTS

KARL RAHNER

BURNS & OATES

Original edition "Kirche und Sakramente" © Herder, Freiburg, 1963
This English version © Search Press and Verlag Herder KG, 1974
Translated by W. J. O'Hara

First published 1963
First published in Great Britain 1974
9th Impression 1986

Nihil Obstat: Joannes M. T. Barton, S.T.D., L.S.S.
Censor deputatus

Imprimatur: †Georgius L. Craven, Epus. Sebastopolis, Vic. Cap.
Westmonasterii, die 7ª Feb., 1963

The Nihil Obstat and Imprimatur are a declaration that a book or pamphlet is considered to be free from doctrinal or moral error. It is not implied that those who have granted the Nihil Obstat and Imprimatur agree with the contents, opinions or statements expressed.

Printed in Great Britain by A. Wheaton & Co. Ltd, Exeter, Devon

ISBN 0 86012 005 8

CONTENTS

Church and Sacraments 9

I. THE CHURCH AS THE CHURCH OF THE
SACRAMENTS 11

  1. The Church as the Fundamental Sacrament . . 11

  2. Explanation of the Sacramental Structure
of the Church and its Actualization in the Seven
Sacraments Generally 20
    a. Various levels of the Church's activity . . 20
    b. The actual fulfilment of the Church's essence
as the sign of an individual's sanctification . . 21

  3. The Nature of a Sacrament in General, Viewed in
Relation to the Church as Fundamental Sacrament 24
    a. *Opus operatum* 24
    b. The reviviscence of the sacraments . . . 33
    c. *Sacramentum* and *res sacramenti* 34
    d. The way the sacraments cause grace . . . 34
    e. The institution of the sacraments by Christ 41
    f. Sacramental and personal piety 74

CONTENTS

II. THE VARIOUS SACRAMENTS AS ACTS IN WHICH THE CHURCH'S NATURE IS FULFILLED.

THE ECCLESIOLOGICAL ASPECT OF THE SACRAMENTS AS EVENTS IN THE INDIVIDUAL'S SANCTIFICATION . . . 76

1. General Considerations 76
2. The Eucharist. 82
3. Baptism 87
4. Confirmation 90
5. Penance 93
6. Holy Order 95
7. Matrimony 107
8. The Anointing of the Sick 112

CHURCH AND SACRAMENTS

THE subject that is to be dealt with in this *Quaestio disputata* is: the Church and the sacraments. The two concepts are intended to throw light on one another in the course of the inquiry, so that a deeper understanding of the Church may be gained by asking what the sacraments are, and greater comprehension of the sacraments, by reflecting on what the Church is. In the mind of the faithful at large, and perhaps even for theologians, the connection between Church and sacraments is not very clear. Everyone knows that the Church is empowered to dispense the sacraments because they were instituted by Christ and their administration entrusted to the Church by her founder. But that is more or less all that is thought of as connecting the two. In general, the sacraments are regarded as means of grace for the salvation of the individual, which they certainly are, of course, but as nothing else. If the sacraments are viewed in that way, the Church can only appear as the dispenser of these means of grace for the individual's salvation, as the supplier of heavenly treasures, as it were, to whom one must turn to obtain them, but from whom one turns away as soon as they have been supplied. In this way the relationship between the two remains so superficial and external that in the average view it would not be at all inconceivable that God might just as well have entrusted the administration of those means of grace to some other person or institution. The Church as Church, and the Church as dispenser of the mysteries of God, are almost only *per accidens* one and the same. If the connection between Church and sacraments is to be more clearly and deeply recognized, it will be necessary to deal first with the Church as the Church of the sacraments, so that the inquiry will proceed from the Church and a correct understanding of what she is, towards the sacraments; and secondly with the various sacraments as the living accomplishment of the Church's nature, so that the relation of each to the Church may be recognized, and as a consequence an understanding of the Church's nature achieved, with the sacraments as starting-point.

I

THE CHURCH AS
THE CHURCH OF THE SACRAMENTS

1. *The Church as the Fundamental Sacrament*

THE Church is not merely a religious institution, established to meet religious needs. It goes without saying that it was not created by men for that purpose. But neither was it simply founded from above by Christ as a spiritual welfare establishment. The institutional, hierarchical build of the Church with its legal and official organization, which, of course, exists and is essential to the Church and shares in the indispensability of the Church for salvation, is the juridical constitution of something that must be already there for it to be given such a constitution. The reality that has to be so organized and constituted, with a basis in a hierarchical and juridical order that is its expression, is not the amorphous mass of individual human beings in need of redemption, but the "people of God". It is because this is what it is, not what it has yet to become, that it receives in the Church as a juridical organization its institutional structure according to Christ's will at its foundation.

Can this be made more precise? A comparison may help. An actual State that has come into existence in the course of history, for all its importance for the life of a nation, is not what first brings together an amorphous mass of individual human beings into a community. It is rather the actual existence of a national group, with a common history, a common territory, a certain historic mission, a common civilization and so on, that brings about the existence of the State. Of course the two things condition one another, for the common cultural life of a single nation and the unity of its history is itself grounded in the existence of a single State, or at least may be. The State exists because logically if not necessarily in time, the nation is prior with its unity of territory, history, civilization and so on.

A similar relation holds between the Church as a juridically organized society and the reality we are calling the "people of God". What is meant by the people of God? The eternal Word of the Father, born of the virgin Mary one of the daughters of Eve, has become of one race and family with us (Heb. 2:11), not merely of the same nature in the abstract as it were. He belongs to the one human race which is not merely the logical sum of the multitude of individual human beings, but an actually real unity by the will of God. However difficult it may be to find categories to define it, this unity is manifested in the monogenetic descent of all men from the one Adam, is raised above nature by the call of all mankind in that one Adam to a supernatural destiny, and unfolds in original sin and the one history of the human race in salvation and perdition. That unity is confirmed, increased and made definitive by the incarnation of the Logos. Since he is man, a human nature is divinized, thanks to the hypostatic union, through the sanctifying grace that necessarily ensues from that union, and shares in the immediate presence of God by direct vision and love. But because this man Jesus is a member of the one human race, this itself is called to a supernatural destiny in and through him, even if it were not so called in Adam, or not called in Adam because called in Christ as first willed by God. God maintains this vocation of all humanity, despite sin, on account of Christ, who by what he is and what he does, the sacrificial death on the cross, is a member of this single human race. God sees all human beings as brothers and sisters of his incarnate Son "in the midst of the Church" (Heb. 2: 10–11), as the people of God with whom he has concluded that new and eternal covenant by that union between God and creature which we call the hypostatic union. By the gracious coming of the Logos in the flesh, in the unity of the race, in the one history of humanity, mankind as a whole has become a consecrated humanity, in fact the people of God.

Even though in biblical as well as in present-day official ecclesiastical terminology "Church" and "Body of Christ" too always signify the society comprising the whole of mankind called to supernatural salvation in Christ, with its juridical build and the hierarchical, social, organized structure given to it by Christ, that does not alter the fact that this organized association of those who are called to redemption, and the personal acceptance of the call by the individual, are in fact preceded, even chronologically, by a consecration of the whole of mankind which took place in the incarnation and death on the cross of the eternal Word of the Father. As the people of God socially and juridically organized, the Church is not a mere eternal welfare institute, but the continuation, the perpetual presence of the task and function of Christ in the economy of redemption, his contemporaneous presence in history, his life, the Church in the full and proper sense. To make this clearer, Christ's own rôle in the mystery of redemption must be considered rather more closely.

Christ is the historically real and actual presence of the eschatologically victorious mercy of God. The incarnation is not merely the constituting of a subject who, if eventually he is willing, or is given the task by God, can intercede for sinful mankind before the holy majesty of God, through an atonement that gives Christ a claim to be heard as of right. If it were, nothing at all would have been determined by the incarnation itself in regard to redemption. The connection between the two realities would only consist in God's having willed the incarnation "in view of" the cross. Such a view cannot do justice to the "physical" theory of the redemption found in the Greek Fathers of the Church nor explain why the hypostatic union continued even after the crucifixion. It also makes it difficult to understand why the redemption actually took place through a sharing in the lot of sinners, suffering the death that is theirs, the very manifestation of their guilt. Rather did God by the incarnation take the world fundamentally and once and for all into his mercy. Through the incarnation the whole of redemption was already pre-formed, even if it still had to be carried out in the suffering of death, precisely because the Logos had assumed the "flesh of sin", as St. Paul says in Romans 8:3, in other words the flesh that is marked out for death, and a true human life that must be personally lived through, not merely a static "nature" that endures without a history. For the Logos redeemed by really identifying himself with the sinner.

Consequently the whole of mankind is in principle already accepted for salvation in this member and head of mankind who is irrevocably united with God in unity of person. From the moment the Logos assumes this human nature from out of the unity of mankind, and as a part of it, redemption cannot be arrested or cancelled. The fate of the world has been finally decided, and in the sense of divine mercy. Before Christ, the dialogue between God and mankind in the history of eternal welfare and loss was an open one, the history of mankind as a whole could lead to salvation or ruin (though that does not imply any clear decision one way or the other for the individual). Everything was still unsettled. New, incalculable and surprising reactions of the living God who manifests himself in his actions throughout that history, could take place. Of what kind they would be, was not to be inferred from the previous course of human history with God. But now in the Word of God, God's last word is uttered into the visible public history of mankind, a word of grace, reconciliation and eternal life: Jesus Christ. The grace of God no longer comes (when it does come) steeply down from on high, from a God absolutely transcending the world, and in a manner that is without history, purely episodic; it is permanently in the world in tangible historical form, established in the flesh of Christ as a part of the world, of humanity and of its very history.

That is what we mean by saying that Christ is the actual historical presence in the world of the eschatologically triumphant mercy of God. It is possible to point to a visible, historically manifest fact, located in space and time, and say, Because that is there, God is reconciled to the world. There the grace of God appears in our world of time and space. There is the spatio-temporal sign that effects what it points to. Christ in his historical existence is both reality and sign, *sacramentum* and *res sacramenti*, of the redemptive grace of God, which through him no longer, as it did before his coming, rules high over the world as the as yet hidden will of the remote, transcendent God, but in him is given and established in the world, and manifested there.

Consequently it would be totally to misapprehend the message of Christianity (yet how often it occurs in preaching), if one were to attempt to think of God's plan of salvation as opening out two possibilities, two ways, between which man's freedom, neutral and indifferent in itself, had to choose: salvation or perdition, God or damnation. Of course, each has freely to decide, and life and death are presented for choice. But God did not simply set up a fully equipped stage, for men to act out the drama of their history on their own. God himself has taken part, acted, given the drama the dénouement he himself wanted: salvation, grace and eternal life. The individual human being cannot, as long as he is a pilgrim and faced with decision, yet say whether and how this one divinely effected consummation of the whole of history will end in blessedness for him. But because he cannot tell that about himself or any other individual, speaking generally, he must not have the impression on that account that history as a whole is still at the disposition of mankind, with God awaiting the decision. History as a whole is already decided, and by God. Not that man's freedom is abolished thereby. But in Christ himself God has decided the free consent of man as a whole in regard to the God of grace and life, in faith and love. In its teaching on grace, theology must not only say, as all its schools of thought do, that God by his efficacious grace "can" decide the free consent of man to his salvation, not abolishing the free consent but constituting it. If it is to do justice to holy Scripture, theology must say, and generally forgets to say, that God has actually promised this efficacious grace for history as a whole and its single end (which can be viewed as the final result and the one meaning and pattern of all human history). When we say that Christ on the cross merited incontestably and irrevocably the "grace of God", that grace is not only to be understood as a "possibility" of effecting redemption, as a mere offer of attaining forgiveness and producing works of eternal life. That grace, viewed in relation to the totality of the history of the world and mankind, is a grace which effects the acceptance of what it offers, for, of course, all is grace, the possibility and the realization of the possibility, the capacity and the act, the word of God and the answer of man. And seeing that this grace with its eschatological invincibility and conclusiveness is given in Christ, and promised to the individual in so far as he belongs to the people of God, the promise and presence of this grace, understood in this way, has a public character, and is not only a factor in the private history of the interior life of the individual.

This last-mentioned characteristic of grace is another thing that needs clarification. There is official, public history and private, individual history. The history of a nation, if it is not given an individualistic and liberalistic misinterpretation, is not simply the sum-total of the individual private lives of the human beings who compose that people. There is also the history of the nation as a nation, as a whole. The same is proportionately true of the sacred history of salvation and eternal loss which unfolds between mankind and God acting in the history of the world. There, too, there is the private history of the individual's grace and sin, and the public, official, "political" (from πόλις) history of humanity and the nations in eternal welfare and ruin, as this is effected by God and by human beings who act as spokesmen for the nations and epochs. Christ belongs to this history, but of course in a way that is his alone. In this dimension of the πολί-τευμα of salvation (citizenship, see Phil. 3:20), Christ is the primal sacramental word of God, uttered in the one history of mankind, in which God made known his irrevocable mercy that cannot be annulled by God or man, and did this by effecting it in Christ, and effected it by making it known.

Now the Church is the continuance, the contemporary presence, of that real, eschatologically triumphant and irrevocably established presence in the world, in Christ, of God's salvific will. The Church is the abiding presence of that primal sacramental word of definitive grace, which Christ is in the world, effecting what is uttered by uttering it in sign. By the very fact of being in that way the enduring presence of Christ in the world, the Church is truly the fundamental sacrament, the well-spring of the sacraments in the strict sense. From Christ the Church has an intrinsically sacramental structure. Historically visible in space and time, with its double aspect as people of God and as juridical and social organization of this people, the Church is the body and bride of Christ who abides in the Church as the presence in the world of God's historical and eschatological promise of himself, during this last of its epochs. He does not abandon the Church, and cannot do so, since he himself wills to remain forever in the flesh of the one human family.

This abiding presence of Christ in the Church is the sign that God in his merciful love identifies himself in Christ with the world. And because the Church is the sign of the grace of God definitively triumphant in the world in Christ, this sign can never — as a real possibility — become a meaningless symbol. As an historical and social entity, the Church is always and unchangeably the sign which brings with it always and inseparably what it signifies. As with Christ the distinction between his Godhead and his humanity remains without confusion though they are inseparable, sign and reality, manifest historical form and Holy Spirit, are not the same in the Church, but as in Christ, are not separable any more either. The Church is the official presence of the grace of Christ in the public history of the one human race. In its socially organized form the people of God as in fact redeemed by Christ, receives his permanent presence through history. And when we examine what this one reality implies, it means a presence, as it were an incarnation, of the truth of Christ in the Church through Scripture, tradition and magisterium; a similar embodiment and presence of Christ's will in the Church's teaching when it announces Christ's precepts in her pastoral office and her constitution; and a presence and embodiment, again analogous to the incarnation, of the grace of Christ, for the individual as such, through the sacraments. Viewed in relation to Christ, the Church is the abiding promulgation of his grace-giving presence in the world. Viewed in relation to the sacraments, the Church is the primal and fundamental sacrament.

2. Explanation of the Sacramental Structure of the Church and its Actualization in the Seven Sacraments Generally

a. Various levels of the Church's activity

The Church is not a mythical entity to be hypostasized or personified in a false way. By the will of Christ her founder she is the organized community of the people of God, established through the incarnation in the unity of the one human race. Even if such a society is represented by individual human beings, it still remains a community. Such a collectivity may in a true sense continue in being even when all its members are asleep and the common business or activity for the moment has completely ceased. But in order to exist, nevertheless, a community has to fulfil its nature, must actually function. The enduring existence of such a society can to be sure find concrete expression in the most diverse ways, and manifest itself with greater or less intensity in visible historical form. And a community of spiritual persons depends much more than a real individual person on such *actus secundi* (operations flowing from a nature and expressing it), because it is only an association. One can confidently say that once a society renounced once and for all its own actualization and functioning, it would by that very fact cease to exist altogether. That holds true of the Church too. The Church exists in the full sense, in the highest degree of actual fulfilment of her nature, by teaching, bearing witness to Christ's truth, bearing the cross of Christ through the ages, loving God in her members, rendering present in rite in the sacrifice of the mass the saving grace that is hers.

b. The actual fulfilment of the Church's essence as the sign of an individual's sanctification

If it is true to say that the Church as the continuance of Christ's presence in the world, is the fundamental sacrament of the eschatologically triumphant mercy of God, then salvation is offered and promised to the individual by his entering into positive relation to the Church. This positive relationship may possibly have very different degrees and grades of intensity, but if the individual is to attain salvation, can never entirely be lacking. God's life is offered to men plainly and once and for all in Christ, through whose incarnation the people of God exists. This has socially organized form in the Church, which is consequently the abiding and historically manifest presence of this saving grace in Christ, the fundamental sacred sign or sacrament of this grace. From this the necessity of the Church for salvation — at root it is the necessity of Christ himself — directly follows. Its necessity as a means is also clear, the kind of necessity which is presupposed by the question of a moral claim to men's obedience. We have also, of course, in the distinction between the aspect: people of God, and the aspect: juridical constitution of that people, within the one complete unity of the Church, an objective means of discerning degrees of intensity in membership of the Church, so that in fact there can be no instance of saving grace of which one would have to say, that it had no connection with the Church and with membership of the Church.[1] So though the individual, in what concerns his own personal sanctification, works out his own unique, irreplaceable salvation in personal freedom, he always

[1] See K. Rahner, *Schriften zur Theologie* II (Einsiedeln ³1958) 7–94.

does so by finding his way to the Church. For the Church is the presence of saving grace in the world. To deny the ecclesiastical character of all grace and redemption would either imply that grace is not always related to the incarnation, to history and so to the Church, or else it would imply that one can attain salvation without the grace of Christ.

If, however, the means of grace, its presence, has a sacramental structure, that is, is based on the unity of grace and its historically manifest concrete embodiment, this must also be true of access to this means or fountain of grace, of entry into it, and of any further acceptance of grace by the individual from it. That does not imply that any and every conferring and acceptance of the grace present in the Church as the fundamental sacrament, has in every case the nature of a sacrament in the strictest and technical sense of the word. It has been sufficiently indicated already, and we cannot go into the matter further here, that any grace-giving event has a quasi-sacramental structure and shares in Christ's character as both divine and human. But when the Church in her official, organized, public capacity precisely as the source of redemptive grace meets the individual in the actual ultimate accomplishment of her nature, there we have sacraments in the proper sense, and they can then be seen to be the essential functions that bring into activity the very essence of the Church herself. For in them she herself attains the highest degree of actualization of what she always is: the presence of redemptive grace for men, historically visible and manifest as the sign of the eschatologically victorious grace of God in the world.

Now if the Church as the people of God in a socially organized form is the enduring historical presence of the eschatologically triumphant grace of God and of Christ in the world for the individual, the obtaining of grace by the individual cannot consist simply in his approval and consent to the mere presence of this redemptive grace. A community with an organized structure only acquires by its own act reality and validity for the individual who at first is outside it. A society must "enrol" him if he is to enter it. It is only in that way, then, that it is manifest that God's redemptive grace in Christ is a free grace, his own operation in us and not a factual reality always of necessity present, and in regard to which it is really only a question for us, of what attitude we choose to adopt towards it. The actualization or accomplishment of the eschatologically victorious redemptive grace established in the Church for the world and offered to all men, takes place, therefore, (in instances where this accomplishment is realized fully and perfectly), in an act of the Church in the individual's regard, whereby the gratuitous character of redemptive grace is proclaimed. This act of the Church in regard to man necessarily bears within it the structure of the Church's own nature. It is sacramental in accordance with the Church's character as the primal sacrament of grace. It is to be remembered here that we have called the Church the fundamental sacrament, not by a vague borrowing of the concept of sacrament known to us already from the current teaching about the sacraments, but by deriving our concept from Christology. Therefore fundamental sacrament means for us the one abiding symbolic presence, similar in structure to the incarnation, of the eschatological redemptive grace of Christ; a presence in which sign and what is signified are united inseparably but without confusion, the grace of God in the "flesh" of an historical and tangible ecclesiastical embodiment, which therefore cannot be emptied of what it signifies and renders present, because otherwise the grace of Christ (who always remains man), would also be something merely transitory and replaceable, and in the last resort we would still be under the old covenant. Consequently, because first of all and independently of the usual idea of a sacrament, we envisage the Church as the fundamental or primal sacrament, and form the root idea of a sacrament in the ordinary sense as an instance of the fullest actualization of the Church's essence as the saving presence of Christ's grace, for the individual, we can in fact obtain from this an understanding of the sacraments in general.

3. *The Nature of a Sacrament in General, Viewed in Relation to the Church as Fundamental Sacrament*

We have, of course, no intention of attempting to deduce in precise detail from this conception all the basic characteristics of the sacraments as they are listed in the treatises on the sacraments in general. Nevertheless a few indications must be given.

a. *Opus operatum*

Our viewpoint permits a deeper understanding of the meaning of *opus operatum*. When applied to one of these acts of the Church in regard to an individual in which her nature is accomplished, this expression simply says what we said about the Church in general when we explained that she is the definitive sign, impossible to deprive of meaning, of God's grace in the world, which is rendered present by being manifested in this way in the Church.

The concept of *opus operatum* is, of course, not as simple as might at first appear. We are leaving out of account the fact that in standard theology it is not identical with the concept of a sacrament, as there are instances of it which are not sacraments (the mass as sacrifice; indulgences too, according to a commonly held view). The idea in itself too presents considerable difficulties which can perhaps be solved more easily with the present approach than if one starts from the individual sacraments themselves and tries to build up the concept of *opus operatum* from them. In the usual account, the concept means that grace is conferred on the recipient through the positing of the sacramental sign itself, and neither the merit (holiness) of the minister nor that of the recipient is causally involved (Denzinger 849, 850f.).

It is explained that God has linked his grace once and for all to the making of this sign and that through this connection established by God himself between sign of grace and grace signified, any objection that the sacramental *opus operatum* is being understood in a magical way *ipso facto* vanishes, all the more so as the need for inner receptiveness and for appropriation in faith of the grace conferred is not only not excluded but is expressly taught by the Council of Trent (Denzinger 797f., 819, 849). All that is correct and at first sight quite clear. But we must note that in the first place the Council teaches the necessity, if the sacrament is to be received with fruit by an adult, of a right disposition: active co-operation in the reception of the sacrament with faith and love. Consequently the sacrament in its concrete reality involves, like the *opus operantis* (the dispositions of the recipient), an element of uncertainty about grace, of doubt about its factual efficacy. With the sacrament a person knows just as little as he does with his merely "subjective" actions performed in faith, whether it has really given him God's grace. Just as little and just as much. That is after all an undeniable fact which is hidden in the popular view of the sacraments by what the average person thinks *opus operatum* implies. Everyone has heard Catholics say, or has himself thought, that when someone prays or repents of his sins, he is not as sure that God has heard him or forgiven him as he is if he goes to the sacraments. Since Scotus more or less, this idea has been one of the standard arguments in apologetics to show the necessity or utility of the sacrament of penance, confession, even when this is not strictly obligatory because no grave sins are in question. The idea of *opus operatum* in fact current, contains an element of what one might almost call physical certainty of functioning, which does not belong to it in more accurate theology. Conversely one can certainly affirm that God has attached the unconditional promise of grace and help to other realities as well as to the sacramental signs. If someone prays in the name of Jesus for saving grace and for nothing else (and in a particular case he knows as much or as little whether he is doing so as he does about his dispositions when he receives the sacraments), he knows with infallible certainty that God hears him, even if perhaps the precise mode of the answer remains hidden and must be left in God's hands. It is not a cogent objection to this example to say that here the prayer as *opus operantis* represents a "merit" and consequently the obtaining of grace and its measure depend on the measure of this subjective merit, whereas fortunately this is excluded in the case of the sacraments, where God acts towards men according to his own generosity and good pleasure. This does not meet the difficulty. For the measure of grace in the sacraments is dependent on the quality of the recipient's dispositions (Denzinger 799).

Furthermore, even if the prayer is meritorious, God's hearing the prayer is not based on the merit that accrues through the prayer, but as all theologians agree, on the fact that in prayer as such, appeal is made for Christ's sake to the infinite generosity of God. It is to this prayer that God has promised an absolutely certain hearing. Consequently one can say in a general way with regard to the two instances that in both of them, the sacrament and the prayer, and not only in the one where we employ the term *opus operatum,* we have occurrences to which, if they are true and genuine, God has absolutely promised his grace. Other acts could be quoted as well as prayer, that have a similar character, and we only omit them because in this connection they occupy a less prominent place in the average Catholic's awareness of his faith: reading of Scripture, listening to the word of God, and others. But in both the instances we are dealing with, grace is also conferred according to the measure of the recipient's dispositions which, of course, in the last resort are themselves a gift of grace. In both cases, too, the operative cause is not really the (supernatural) merit of man (which exists) but God's promise. So where is the real difference between the *opus operatum* of the sacraments and these other instances of grace being conferred, which we do not call sacraments?

In order to be in a position later to give as concrete an answer as possible to this question, let us illustrate once more with an example. Someone repents of his sins with genuine contrition and conversion, in his own conscience. If he does this, he knows with absolute certainty, by reason of the faithful and irrevocable words of the divine promise, that God truly forgives him his guilt. What happens then is an actual instance of grace being conferred, not a merely "subjective" desire for it to happen. Another man confesses his sins contritely in the sacrament of penance. He knows that God forgives him his guilt by the

Church's power of the keys, if he is truly and genuinely repentant. In neither case is there absolute certainty about the fulfilment of the condition. In both cases, over and above what the man does and experiences, he must also trust in God and his inscrutable judgment, seeing that in both cases he is obliged to trust firmly and unshakenly (not to know), with simple and childlike hope, (for God is greater than our heart), that God will truly have produced by his grace the necessary condition, our "good will". In the first case we speak of *opus operantis,* in the second of *opus operatum.* What is the difference between the two?

First of all it must be calmly and candidly recognized that the difference is not at all as radical as a rather mediocre theology would have it. Supernatural activity where grace is conferred and promised to us by God, infallibly on his part, and sacramental activity, are not identical. The second is only one of the possible kinds of the first. And as regards our question itself, the answer can only be that in the first case the sign (the prayer, repentance, in other words what the individual as such privately does), to which God has attached his grace, is itself intrinsically fragile, vulnerable, capable that is of becoming invalid of itself, and of being for its own part deprived of the character of visible expression of God's promise of grace. In the second case the sign has an irrevocable eschatological validity; in itself it is the sign of the eternal irrevocable covenant of God with men, a sign which so shares in the eternity and irrevocability of God's salvific will, that the sign itself can never lose the quality of being the visible expression of God's consenting answer to man. It can meet with refusal from man, who can reject the word of God and let it stand against him. But since Christ, and only since him, man can no longer prevent this word's being permanently addressed to him, calling him and not being withdrawn; or that this word summoning him to grace is irrevocably present in the sacramental sign, inseparable from it.

What that implies becomes even clearer if we reflect on the sacraments of the old Law which, according to the Church's teaching, truly existed. Since Augustine, with a few evanescent exceptions, theology has held firmly to their existence and the Church presupposes it in many doctrinal pronouncements (Denzinger 695, 711f., 845, 857). The question therefore arises whether and how they differ from the sacraments of the new covenant. In answering this question theologians got into very obvious difficulties. Particularly in view of the Epistle to the Hebrews, they could not and did not try to locate the difference in the outer form of the rites alone. Such a distinction is clearly too slight and would not do justice to the absolute originality and finality of the new and eternal covenant (Denzinger 845). On the other hand, theology could not be satisfied with the thought of the Epistle to the Hebrews alone, that the Old Testament rites only and exclusively concerned an external ritual "holiness" and were of absolutely no importance for the inner sanctification of men. Of course they were primarily and directly concerned with the "flesh", by the very fact that they had a nationally restricted and earthly import, like the old covenant in general, of which they were the visible expression and realization. As, however, that covenant despite its fleshly character had justification and redemption as its ultimate meaning, for even in the old Law, as the Epistle to the Hebrews also teaches, faith and justification were given by the Spirit of God, so that we have to follow the "father of those who believe" and the "cloud of witnesses" and attain justification and sanctification thereby; and as that giving of grace and the visible covenant with its rites of circumcision and so on were not merely facts juxtaposed in time and space without intrinsic connection, for in that case there would have been no difference at all between the men of the Old Testament and the heathen in the actual workings of grace, and the visible alliance would have been a mere political and national affair, traditional theology with few exceptions has always held that for example circumcision and justification were connected in the old covenant.

On this supposition the problem arises in its full difficulty of how to determine in what the difference between the sacraments of the old Law and the new actually consists, for it is an essential difference. The question becomes even more puzzling when we recall that for a modern treatment in apologetics of the sacramental element in the Church, it is more a question of showing that there have always been sacraments everywhere in the sacred history of redemption, and for that reason theology rightly speaks of *sacramenta legis naturae,* not recognizing any period at which there were no sacraments at all in existence. There is no question of making such apologetics easier by simply referring to a free decree of God instituting as a matter of fact, though doubtless very wisely, sacraments in the new covenant although it need not have been so. Such a theology of mere divine decrees is at bottom a refusal really to think theologically, and it abandons all hope of real apologetics. Without realizing it, such an attitude attributes to the people of to-day an anthropomorphic conception of God, because it thinks of him as ordering now this, now that within the world, whereas after all he freely created a world with definite structures. Once this whole is freely set in being, it is intrinsically coherent. If it is involved in an historical process, and alters, these changes are the fulfilment of the enduring structures of the whole, even if in certain circumstances it is only from the complete accomplishment that the disposition of an earlier stage in view of a later can be recognized, and this recognition is not possible on the basis of the potentialities of the earlier stage alone.

This general consideration shows that it is not to be expected that there was once a time in which no such things as sacraments existed. Such a view or tacit assumption would inevitably make an intelligible apologetics of the sacramental aspect of Christianity extremely difficult. But if there were always things of the sacramental kind, that is, historical spatio-temporal phenomena manifesting the salvific action of God in the individual, the question becomes even more pressing how the sacraments of the new law differ intelligibly from those of pre-Christian times. From all this the answer given to an earlier question will be clearer. The old covenant as such — and the same applies *a fortiori* to all sacred signs under the "law of nature" — was intrinsically fragile; of itself it was transitory, temporary, replaceable and destructible, though capable of persisting outwardly when in truth it had ceased to exist. If it does persist outwardly, though already in fact abolished, through the defection of the nation and the conclusion of the new and eternal covenant, then the signs of grace which were the effective expressions of the alliance, circumcision, the sacrifices and so on, still exist in certain circumstances of course, but in truth are no longer promises of divine grace. That is impossible in the new and eternal covenant, which is the covenant of the visible manifestation of the final grace of God, grace which is God's eschatological victory over the inner fragility of all that is human, even what is divinely established in man. Consequently the signs of grace in the new covenant are always and permanently assurances of divine grace. To be sure they can be refused by the individual as an individual. But they remain the valid and validly promulgated offer of redemption by God. They are truly *opus operatum*. They can only be so when the signs are posited as signs of the Church as such, when they are ultimately and radically the actual accomplishment of the eternal covenant, operations in which the whole nature of this is actualized, for it alone has this assurance and guarantee.

An historically tangible concrete act of a human being, a prayer for instance, does not in itself possess this, because of itself it can be empty of the content that of itself it expresses, and because it is not an act that is accomplished by the Church as such. In such instances one can always say no more than: If this concrete phenomenon really contains what it purports to contain, then the grace of God is bestowed. With the sacraments of the new law, however, one can say unconditionally: Here in all truth a manifestation of God and his salvific will is taking place. It may remain questionable whether here and now grace is received. But it is not questionable that in general grace is in fact received under these signs, for the Church as a whole has also the promise of her own subjective holiness produced and preserved by efficacious grace. Above all, it is not questionable that God here and now in the sacrament offers his grace. Consequently *opus operatum* means the unambiguous, abiding promise irrevocably made by God, and as such recognizable and historically manifest, of grace for the individual human being, a promise made by the God of the new and eternal covenant. The statement that it is a conferring of God's grace without the subjective merit of the minister or the recipient of the sign, is only the negative and therefore secondary formulation of this positive content of the concept.

b. The reviviscence of the sacraments

With our approach it is also possible to understand what theologians teach about the "reviviscence" of the sacraments. It is not a question of a coming to life again, but of a sacramental sign's becoming effective; it still persists with its signification, an irrevocable word of God addressed to the individual, because the human being actually does accept it within the span of time in which, from the nature of the sign, we must consider the proffer of grace still subsists. This varies with each sacramental sign because of the different meaning of each. By its very nature a meal lasts a shorter time than the period of validity of a rite of admission, of the conferring of an office, of the bond of marriage, of the anointing in an illness that puts a human life in jeopardy. On that basis we can understand the distinctions that theologians make concerning the reviviscence of the various sacraments in particular. The reviviscence of the sacraments is simply a property that accompanies their character of being each an *opus operatum*. And *opus operatum* is only the plainest expression in Catholic dogmatic theology to affirm that God gives his grace of himself, on his own initiative; man's answer is truly only an answer, deriving its whole meaning and existence from God's word to man. It is quite surprising that this expression has provoked such contradiction in Protestant theology. *Opus operatum* is not a concept in opposition to faith. It states that God *sola gratia*, out of pure grace, gives this faith and utters this gracious summons to man plainly and simply in the historically visible form of the sacraments. *Opus operatum,* of course, does not mean that where a human being is capable of personal faith, this grace which is offered and unconditionally promised in the sacraments, ignores the faith of the human being. On the contrary, the grace is a grace of faith and love, the grace to be able and to accomplish, a grace which is realized in the loving faith of man.

c. *Sacramentum* and *res sacramenti*

With the approach that takes the Church as starting-point, it is possible to make it clearer how in the sacraments there is the duality of sign and what it signifies, *sacramentum* and *res sacramenti*. Precisely this duality has in fact been indicated in the Church.

d. The way the sacraments cause grace

With the same approach it would be possible to make it comprehensible that the efficacy of the sacraments is precisely that of signs: by signifying, to effect what is signified. For we have already seen that the Church is the visible outward expression of grace, not in the sense that she subsequently announces as it were the presence of something already there without the announcement, but in the sense that in the Church God's grace is given expression and embodiment and symbolized, and by being so embodied, is present. With that in mind it would probably be possible to attain a viewpoint that would put into perspective the controversies, usually so inextricable, concerning the correct theory of the causal efficacy of the sacraments. This much-discussed question is not to be treated again here *in extenso*. We can only give a few indications of how an intelligible approach to a solution of the problem of the nature of sacramental causality can be discerned in the ecclesiological origin of the sacraments.

Usually the question of the kind of causality at work in the sacraments is envisaged unconsciously, as though as a matter of course, in terms of the concept of transitive efficient cause borrowed from the philosophic doctrine of the categories. God, sacramental sign and grace are envisaged from the start as quite distinct factors, almost as though they were material things. Then the causality of the sacramental signs is thought of in relation to God, as a "moral" causality, analogous to that of prayer, for example, the making good of a legal claim on someone who has contracted to perform something. Or it is thought of in terms of grace, and then the efficacy is represented on the analogy of the physical causation of an effect. In view of the difficulty of a rite "physically" causing interior grace, this view calls to its aid the proposition that the causality in question is "instrumental". But then the present-day theory, as opposed to that of some mediaeval theologians who spoke of the production of an *ornatus animae* by way of dispositions in view of the effect, no longer makes it really clear, what precisely it is that even an instrumental cause must itself contribute to the final total effect, for the co-operation of such an instrumental cause to be at all intelligible. Or else the causality of the rite viewed directly in relation to grace, is interpreted in a juridical, "intentional" sense, physical causality being rejected. The sacrament is considered to confer on the recipient a legal title, which may be identical with the sacramental "character" but need not be. It

35

may be wondered whether this theory does not really amount to the same as the *ornatus* theory of the mediaevals, or would do so, if it were interpreted in not too physical a sense.

In all these theories it is noteworthy that the fact that the sacraments are signs plays no part in explaining their causality. Their function as signs and their function as causes are juxtaposed without connection. The axiom everywhere quoted, *sacramenta significando efficiunt gratiam,* is not in fact taken seriously. Nor do these theories take into account the fundamentally human element in the sacraments as sacred rites which have a past and a background in the whole history of man's religious activity. Always and everywhere men have had the conviction that in gestures and rites and figurative representation, what is signified and pointed to, is in fact present, precisely because it is "represented", and this conviction should not be rejected off-hand as "analogy magic".[2] The intrinsic difficulties of these current theories are too well-known for them to need long discussion. "Physical" causality inevitably does most to push the symbolic character of the sacraments into the background. It explains the possibility of reviviscence of the sacraments only with the help of very intricate supplementary hypotheses. It can give no real meaning to the instrumentality of the sacraments, cannot explain what the instrument itself can contribute to the effect, grace, nor make it intelligible how precisely a "symbol" can be the physical instrument of supernatural grace. That theory overlooks that a sign itself is not a "physical" thing, especially as in the sacraments it is composed of words

---

[2] This rejection is false because it fails to recognize the primarily ontological nature of symbol. See K. Rahner, *Theologie des Symbols* (*Schriften zur Theologie* IV, Einsiedeln 1960).

and ritual gestures which themselves are separated in time or form an essentially juridical process, which after all by its very nature cannot be a physical instrument in the same way as water, for instance absolution, or the marriage contract. The theory of "moral" causality, whether it admits it or not, must acknowledge a causality in regard to God which is then retracted by explaining that the real nexus is that between sign and grace: God wills the grace as dependent on the sign, but does not will this grace because of that sign. But, of course, the sign is the cause of grace, not of God's decision physically to confer grace. The theory of "intentional" causality either stops where the question recurs, how the legal title conferred on the recipient of the sacraments itself produces grace, or else it relapses into the theory of moral causality, which it was designed to avoid, when it thinks of the legal title to grace as "moving" God to confer grace. Furthermore the sign in the sacrament precisely as sign is just as unrecognized as it is in the other theories. The fundamental defect that leads all these theories into conceptual difficulties, consists, as we have said, in tacitly laying down the pattern of transitive efficient causality, in which one factor adequately distinct from another must produce the latter.

With the approach we have been using, it can become clear that the sacraments precisely as signs are causes of grace, that it is a case here of causation by symbols, of the kind that belongs to what by its very nature is a symbol. By such "natural symbols" or intrinsically real symbols, we mean for our purpose here, the spatio-temporal, historical phenomenon, the visible and tangible form in which something that appears, notifies its presence, and by so doing, makes itself present, bodying forth this manifestation really distinct from itself. With natural symbols, the sign or symbol as a phenomenon is intrinsically linked to what it is a phenomenon of, and which is present and operative, even though really distinct. In fact we must distinguish between two aspects: the dependence of the actual manifestation on what is manifesting itself, and the difference between the two. To cite a comparable relationship, a spiritual being is an intellectual substance, yet only constitutes itself as such, as mind, by there emanating from it what is not identical with itself, its really distinct power of knowing. A proportionately similar relation holds between phenomenon and underlying reality. Hence it is possible to perceive why the symbol can be really distinct from what is symbolized and yet an intrinsic factor of what is symbolized, essentially related to it. In the same way there holds between what we have called an intrinsic or natural symbol and what it signifies neither a nexus of transitive efficient causality, nor the relation of subsequent notification of something that has already taken place and is in being, by an extrinsic announcement of the state of affairs which is quite unaffected by it. It is a case of an intrinsic and mutual causal relationship. What is manifesting itself posits its own identity and existence by manifesting itself in this manifestation which is distinct from itself. An example of this relationship is available for the scholastic philosopher in the relation between soul and body. The body is the manifestation of the soul, through which and in which the soul realizes its own essence. The sign is therefore a cause of what it signifies by being the way in which what is signified effects itself. The kind of causality expressed in such a conception of symbolism occurs on various levels of human reality. In substantial being (body as the sign or symbol of the soul); in the sphere of activity (bodily gesture through which the inner attitude itself which is expressed by it first attains its own full depth). On this level of activity the informative expression, without prejudice to its essential connection with what is expressed, may be posited quite freely and take the form of a legal reality. When, for example, what is signified is itself freely posited, the sign can share this characteristic. In other words, even a sign freely posited and belonging to a juridical order can be what we have called an intrinsic or essential symbol.

This concept of the intrinsic symbol, though developed so briefly here, must now be employed if we are to grasp what characterizes sacramental causation, and if we are to do this on the basis of the ecclesiological origin of the sacraments. The Church in her visible historical form is herself an intrinsic symbol of the eschatologically triumphant grace of God; in that spatio-temporal visible form, this grace is made present. And because the sacraments are the actual fulfilment, the actualization of the Church's very nature, in regard to individual men, precisely in as much as the Church's whole reality is to be the real presence of God's grace, as the new covenant, these sacramental signs are efficacious. Their efficacy is that of the intrinsic symbol. Christ acts through the Church in regard to an individual human being, by giving his action spatio-temporal embodiment by having the gift of his grace manifested in the sacrament. This visible form is itself an effect of the coming of grace; it is there because God is gracious to men; and in this self-embodiment of grace, grace itself occurs. The sacramental sign is cause of grace in as much as grace is conferred by being signified. And this presence (by signifying) of grace in the sacraments is simply the actuality of the Church herself as the visible manifestation of grace. Consequently the converse holds. The relation between the Church as the historical visible manifestation of grace and grace itself, one of reciprocal conditioning, extends into the relation between sacramental sign and grace conferred. The sign effects grace, by grace producing the sacrament as sign of the sanctification effected. This, of course, can only be said if the Church as an entity is truly and inseparably connected with grace. Only then is her act, when it is an unconditional realization of her essence, (that is of the Church as the presence of grace), essentially and irrevocably a manifestation of grace, so that the manifestation necessarily renders present what is manifested.

This accounts for the connection between *opus operatum* and the causality of the sacraments in relation to grace. Both are rooted in the same nature of the Church as the essentially primal symbol of grace inseparable from what is symbolized (grace).

This kind of causation is sufficient in this matter. All theologians agree that one satisfies the Church's doctrine that the sacraments are a "cause" of grace, provided one holds firmly that grace is conferred "on account of" the sacramental sign. No more is defined, and even the theory that the sacraments are only *condiciones* of the conferring of grace has never been officially rejected. Our interpretation fits all this. Provided the sign is an effect of God the dispenser of grace, it is true to say: This grace is conferred here and now because embodied, and by taking concrete form, in the sacramental manifestation. This statement is not falsified by there being other instances of the conferring of grace in which such sacramental embodiment does not occur. Even in regard to the grace conferred the two kinds, sacramental and non-sacramental, are not identical.

e. The institution of the sacraments by Christ

From the principle that the Church is the primal sacrament it would be possible to see that the existence of true sacraments in the strictest traditional sense is not necessarily and always based on a definite statement, which has been preserved or is presumed to have existed, in which the historical Jesus Christ explicitly spoke about a certain definite sacrament. This would have its importance for apologetics of a less anxious and worried kind in the history of dogma, in the matter of the institution of all the sacraments by Christ. A fundamental act of the Church in an individual's regard, in situations that are decisive for him, an act which truly involves the nature of the Church as the historical, eschatological presence of redemptive grace, is *ipso facto* a sacrament, even if it were only later that reflection was directed to its sacramental character that follows from its connection with the nature of the Church. The institution of a sacrament can (it is not necessarily implied that it must always) follow simply from the fact that Christ founded the Church with its sacramental nature. It is clear too that, properly understood, the treatise *De sacramentis in genere* is not an abstract formulation of the nature of the individual sacraments, but a part of the treatise *De ecclesia*. It rightly precedes doctrine about the individual sacraments; it does not follow as a subsequent secondary generalization; for only on the basis of the doctrine about the Church, the fundamental sacrament, can the sacramentality of several sacraments be recognized at all.

In order to be clear about scope and significance of what for the moment has only been indicated here, we must ask how it is possible to demonstrate in an historically credible way the sacramentality of matrimony, holy order, extreme unction and confirmation, that is to say, here, their institution by Christ, which is, of course, a dogma (Denzinger 844). We have no sayings of Jesus about these sacraments. The authorization given to the apostles to celebrate the Lord's supper is not the institution of a sacramental rite which confers ministry and office. For no one can deny that in the new covenant there are official powers by divine law, and the transmission of such powers, which are not sacraments. One has only to think of Peter and his successors. The sacrament of order does not therefore follow from the *anamnesis* precept, the command to commemorate. Consequently, for four sacraments we have no words of institution from Jesus Christ himself.

Is it historically probable that Christ actually spoke such words though they may not have been handed down to us? Many theologians presume so, and point to the Easter period when the Lord spoke with his apostles concerning the kingdom of God (Acts 1:3). Yet the question cannot be settled by such a general presumption. As there was no general concept of a sacrament at that time, it is in the first place historically plain as a matter of course that Jesus cannot have spoken about these other rites in terms of the concept of sacrament as such. But then the question arises how, if we suppose him to have spoken explicitly, of matrimony, order, etc., he could have spoken so that grace could be recognized as the effect of the events in question. With baptism, for instance, the matter is easy to understand. It is expressly called re-birth, forgiveness of sins, because without these designations it can hardly be intelligibly described even in externals. Similarly with reconciliation with the Church (binding and loosing) and the Lord's supper as the sharing in the redemptive death of Jesus by the *anamnesis* of his passion. In these rites, then, the mention and designation of the rite necessitates the indication of an effect, which is grace. And so a sacrament can be affirmed without more ado from the facts of the case.

But this obvious quality is not present with order and matrimony. It is possible to speak of them intelligibly without any mention of grace being conferred. For one can talk of marriage, its purpose and obligations, its dangers and other characteristics – Jesus Christ did so – without reflecting on the fact that it is an efficacious sign of grace *ex opere operato,* a sacrament. The same is true of the ecclesiastical ministry and its transmission. Ministry is not grace. Consequently it is possible to speak of ministry in the Church and its transmission without saying that the ritual transmission of ministry in the Church is a sign that confers "grace". It follows that when Jesus Christ spoke of the ministry and of marriage, the situation with regard to an explanation of their sacramental quality was different from what it was with baptism, penance and the Lord's supper. He would have had to say something himself in addition. Is it likely? If someone objects: Why shouldn't Christ have done so? two points must be made.

First, how is this supplementary explanation that the well-known ordinary occurrences of contracting marriage or of appointment to office in the community, are also things that confer grace, just like baptism, eucharist and reception back into the community of the redeemed, supposed to have been worded, in expressions that can be supposed to have been spoken by the historical Jesus? If one simply takes as starting-point the divine omniscience of the Logos, one can, of course, consider every concept and every sentence of such an assertion to have been possible for him. But if one starts with the historical Jesus, and one must if one does not wish, without realizing it, to be a theological Monophysite or Docetist, the material of concepts and ideas in which the presumed explanation is supposed to have been given must to some extent be discoverable within the surroundings, thought and manner of expression of Jesus as we know them elsewhere to have been. Otherwise the statement assumed to have been made by Jesus Christ is simply a quite unhistorical postulate. Hence until proof of the contrary, until it is shown that Jesus Christ can be thought to have expressly asserted the sacramentality of matrimony and order more or less in this or that definite way, it becomes historically improbable that Jesus could have explicitly said essentially more than we in fact know him to have done.

Furthermore, if the attempt were made to produce this missing counter-proof, if it were shown that Christ could have said more than tradition has preserved, if it were proved, for example, that his ideas about his Church, of the final and eternal covenant, of the holiness of the new community of the alliance, of the demands made by the ministry on those who share in it, imply that the transmission of ministry must be something of the kind that we nowadays call a sacrament, and that such a statement lay within the possible range of Christ's conceptions and declarations, then precisely the opposite of what was intended has been proved. For one is demonstrating that from what Jesus Christ said in so many words, provided the whole of what he actually said is taken at its full value, the sacramentality of holy order and matrimony can be recognized, and that for that very reason an explicit explanation by Jesus himself is not at all possible and therefore need not necessarily be postulated.

THE CHURCH AS THE CHURCH OF THE SACRAMENTS

The second counter-question is even more important. What is the use of such an explicit statement of Christ about the sacramentality of order and matrimony to be? It only has point to postulate such a saying if it could make it historically likely that the Church recognized the sacramental nature of these transactions because of this saying of Christ. But this is just what cannot seriously be maintained, and must be flatly disputed. Historically speaking, it is quite a naïve way of imagining things, to suppose that these words of Jesus were handed down, orally perhaps, parallel to Scripture and without connection with it, later to become the *dicta probantia* of the explicit knowledge by the Church of the sacramentality of the two sacraments in question.

If we survey the first three or four centuries of theology in the Church, especially regarding marriage, we can quite definitely say that there is not the slightest historical reason to suppose that the Church explicitly knew more then, than is available to us today in all the sources to which we still have access. One may make, if one wishes, the supposition that the sources available to us now from a shorter period of time, the first century and the first half of the second century, for example, no longer inform us of everything that was then known, thought and taught in the Church. Even then one might ask whether it is possible for there to be missing from the sum of these indubitably fragmentary sources anything which the Church of that period taught as a binding truth of the faith; and one could give a negative answer for several reasons. But in any case, in view of the wealth of source material for the first four centuries as a whole, and considering the fact that without any calculation or planning much of the literature that did exist has survived, nothing being deliberately suppressed, we know we have a sample that can be taken as representative of the whole, and therefore it is historically quite unthinkable that any important matters of the kind that were taught as binding truths of faith received from the apostles (note the proviso), are missing for us from the literature of the first four centuries, but were once expressly contained in it. What is no longer available to us in explicit statements concerning binding truths of faith – obviously matters of importance – in this literature, was not present and available in such statements in the first four centuries either. If the attempt is made to find an explicit statement about the sacramentality of marriage in what is said explicitly about marriage in the first four centuries (the time limit is arbitrary, one could extend it much farther), it is a waste of time. A lot will be found about the meaning, divine origin and holiness of marriage, the need of grace for Christian married life, the symbolism of marriage in regard to the relation between Christ and the Church, and so on. But none of this is an explicit assertion of the sacramentality of marriage. Consequently there were no such assertions.

All attempts to give historical verisimilitude to the contrary view would amount, as in the case of the supposed words of Christ, to showing that in the actually surviving words of the Fathers, the present teaching about the sacramentality of marriage is implicitly contained, in other words all such attempts would in fact prove the opposite of what was intended. For these explanatory attempts all involve a supplementary general principle, and so the further question arises of what this principle is and how it is known to be valid. A reply to that question, however, leads to considerations which in fact point in the direction which we are following here; in other words it becomes clear that the general principles were already known all the time, and so there was no need and is no need today to argue from an explicit statement of Christ about the sacramentality of marriage.

If that is so, what would be the point of the explicit statement of Christ about the sacramentality of marriage? Historically it is not available. It has not been handed down. It had no influence on doctrine even in the early Church. Even if, contrary to all historical probability it is postulated, it contributes nothing to the purpose for which it is adduced, that is, to explain how and by what means the Church knows about the sacramentality of marriage. Even if Christ's saying existed, the Church must have recognized this sacramentality from another source.

What is said in the fifth chapter of Ephesians makes no essential difference to this state of affairs. The Council of Trent (Denzinger 969) says cautiously that Paul in that passage "suggests" *(innuit)* the sacramentality of marriage. But that means after all that it has to be deduced from the passage. It can only be inferred by introducing many other considerations and truths which are also contained in revelation as a whole. It can only be deduced with the help of a conceptual apparatus which had first to be formed in a slow process of historical development. If according to the Council Paul in this passage only "suggests", "hints at", it certainly does not mean that he explicitly knew more about this question and simply contented himself in this passage with a passing allusion, but in other contexts no longer available to us, said substantially more. Such an affirmation presupposes exactly the same historical improbabilities that we have noted in the similar hypothesis of a saying of Christ, once explicitly made but no longer preserved.

It will have to be left till later to discuss in greater detail how, if all this is presupposed, the sacramentality of marriage is nevertheless to be established, on the basis of the doctrine that the Church is the primal sacrament and that the character of being an *opus operatum* belongs to all her fundamental actions in regard to the individual in which she accomplishes her very nature as ultimate sacrament in situations that are decisive for the individual's spiritual life. This is best done in connection with the question of the ecclesiological aspect of marriage, that is, in the second part of this essay.

If the problem arises in the case of one sacrament, that it cannot be conceived as coming into existence through an actual formal statement of Christ instituting it, and yet must have been instituted by him, then the problem arises generally. There is no reason why the same possibility should not be reckoned with as with marriage (that is, that their institution by our Lord was of the kind we have already referred to but still have to make clear), in cases where such words of institution are perhaps less improbable, but have not really been shown to exist, and cannot positively be represented as historically probable.

That is true in the first place of holy order. Jesus established a ministry in the Church. But no word of his concerning its sacramental nature has been handed down to us. That he uttered such a word, nevertheless, is not to be deduced from the fact that in the Jerusalem community and then in Paul's churches this ministry was already transmitted by a rite of imposition of hands. That gesture was one used even before the Christian era, as a ritual for the handing on of office. It was quite a matter of course for it to be employed in handing on official Christian authority too. And it was just as much a matter of course if the transmission or conferring of office was looked upon as that and nothing else. But in our current text-books it is said that it is plain to be seen in the theology of the Pastoral Epistles that this rite of conferring the ministry is also declared to confer grace, and that this could not have been known without an explicit statement by Christ, for no one but God the giver of grace and Christ whom he sent, could link grace to a rite as its effect. Consequently it is certain that Christ instituted holy order as a sacrament by his word, that is, by an express statement to the apostles. Not all of this argument is sound. In the first place it is not at all so easy to show, if one argues only from the texts directly concerned, that the connection between the rite of conferring ministry, and grace, is meant to be as close and certain as the above argument supposes. Why should this connection not have been thought of as, to use the modern term, a "sacramental"?

In the piety of all ages there have been many rites thought to confer grace, yet without its being possible to declare that they were sacraments: imposition of hands, blessings and so on. If it is said that the more detailed correct interpretation could only be recognized unmistakably and with certainty through tradition, in other words through the later declarations of the Church's magisterium, but that this does not prevent the texts being understood as pointing in the same direction, the question must be put in return, what was the source of this supplementary knowledge displayed in later teaching and going beyond the minimum, inescapable sense of the texts? Unless one is going to answer this by alluding to the infallible assistance of the Holy Spirit (which simply amounts to declaring an answer impossible within the domain of theological argument, and so closing the debate on rather easy terms), a solution can only be looked for in the direction in which all our reflections on the establishment of some of the sacraments by Christ tend.

Secondly the preferred explanation presupposes the point to be proved, which isn't proved, and the contrary of which can be held without anxiety. It implies in fact that the linking with sanctifying grace of a ritual imposition of hands conferring office, can only be known by the apostles or the later Church, through an explicit statement of Christ concerning precisely this fact. But it is just this assumption which is unproved and incorrect, as can be seen from the possible manner of institution of a sacrament by Christ which we have suggested, namely by implicit institution of a sacrament in the explicit instituting of the Church as the historically visible form of eschatologically victorious grace. As with matrimony, we postpone to the second part of this essay the question how in these conditions the sacramentality of order, which as a "ministry" was explicitly established by Christ, can be proved, on the basis that the Church is the fundamental sacrament and that the *opus operatum* is the radical self-expression and actualization of this Church.

If one can reasonably ask in the case of marriage and also of holy order, whether it is historically probable that these two sacraments were instituted by an express statement of Christ, and incline to a negative answer because explicit words of institution of that kind are historically very unlikely in regard to the first and in the case of the second cannot be shown to have any positive likelihood, then the same question can also be put regarding confirmation and extreme unction. Not that it should be presupposed *a priori* that all the sacraments are in the same case. Indeed it is a defect in our usual theology of the sacraments that, because there are seven, they are all given the same stamp, whether it is a matter of proving their existence or of discussing their nature. And in fact with these two sacraments the situation is different when they are compared with one another or with the other sacraments. Yet on closer examination the question of how they were instituted points in the same direction as before.

As regards confirmation, its whole history indicates how closely it belongs with baptism, as a part of Christian initiation. Certainly we may not affirm, nor does history oblige us to, that confirmation is not a sacrament because it stands in particularly close connection with baptism or because in the Acts of the Apostles it looks as if confirmation had split off from baptism. (Though confirmation was administered in Samaria, one has not the impression that anything was lacking to "baptism" in Jerusalem. The Holy Spirit was received here by a man's cleansing from sins by baptism and incorporation in faith into the new people of God, in which the Holy Spirit was poured out, so that he filled everyone who was admitted.) But why should not we be able to say that the fact of incorporation into the people of the new covenant is forgiveness of sins and infusion of the Spirit? Why then could we not add that this one incorporation takes place, though it is one, through two rites, which in their duality represent and effect the two sides of the one process, death to the past and the old adam (forgiveness of sins), and new life (gift of the Spirit)? Why should each part of the one event not be called a sacrament? Why then not two sacraments be spoken of? Every theological theory speaks of a general grace common to the sacraments, without anyone thinking the plurality of the sacraments endangered thereby. The particular grace that characterizes and distinguishes each of them is reasonably understood to be, not an extrinsic supplement to the general grace, but an intrinsic specialization of the one grace of the sacraments which can cause its manifold vital energies to operate in the most diverse directions. If that is correct, the sacraments are distinguished from one another not only by the outward rites but by their effects also, but this difference of effect is not a difference between things that are simply disparate. It is the difference which one and the same gift, grace, has and can have in the development of its own dynamic force. Even if it is given primarily with a certain orientation, at the same time it contains virtually the potentialities of the other dynamic forces of the one grace.

It will be noted we are speaking of sacramental grace, not of orders as such or marriage as such. So it is, for example, that the eucharist can *per accidens* give the grace of justification and extreme unction forgiveness of sins. It is therefore possible that by baptism itself (as distinct from confirmation), one is incorporated into the Church, and possesses the Spirit and yet that the giving of the Spirit in contradistinction to the forgiveness of sins is signified and effected through another rite. And the identity in the potentiality of the one grace (for all the difference in direction of its actualization) need not oppose the duality of the sacraments. That must be said quite independently of the question how explicitly or implicitly both sacraments were instituted by Christ. Everyone who knows how difficult it is, in Scripture, in tradition and in present-day dogmatic theology too, to distinguish between the sacramental grace of these two sacraments, also knows that it is really an impossible undertaking if one takes distinguishing them to imply that one of these two sacraments does not give implicitly and virtually simply what the other gives explicitly, actually and more abundantly. If one were to try to distinguish them, the gift of the Spirit in confirmation could only be understood as something very incidental, instead of being the messianic gift of possession of the Holy Spirit, as the sources after all require us to understand it. With that view of the effect of confirmation, however, one cannot, in accordance with Scripture in other contexts, refuse the same effect to baptism itself, all the more so as, if one did, one would be denying that baptism alone can be sufficient for salvation. One can be saved by baptism alone, yet no one can reach heaven who does not possess the Spirit. In any case, if the two sacraments do stand in the relation of two sacramental phases of a single process, intrinsically one yet having several aspects, and which can be articulated even in time in their visible sacramental form and their effects, without detriment to the unity of the process which washes away sins, gives the Spirit and incorporates into the community of the redeemed, then one can also say that the complete meaning of the one full initiation into the Church is represented with its two aspects in two different rites, which were distinguished by the Church of the apostles, and that both of them can be called sacraments, without its being necessary that Christ himself must have explicitly prescribed this division of the rite into two. Moreover, one will not on that account have denied that Christ instituted both sacraments in the one whole that the initiation forms.

It is not difficult to grasp how this ritual distribution of the initiation instituted by Christ (in instituting the Church and baptism), came about. "Baptism" at that time, especially with the baptism of John in men's minds, must have predominantly had the meaning of a remission of sins, a baptism of penance. One cannot, of course, assume the whole Pauline theology of death and resurrection with Christ to have been explicitly contained in their rite in the original community in Jerusalem, if only for the reason that Paul in his theology of baptism is thinking of the whole rite of initiation. From Acts 19 we can see that he very likely conferred confirmation at the same time and so in passages like Romans 6 he is including under "baptism" this part of the initiation too. Consequently when in the original Jerusalem community they wanted to say in so many words that baptism is not only received as a baptism of penance when one enters Christ's Church in accordance with his will, but that with the Church and with membership of the Church the fullness of the Spirit is given, this was best done by adding to the washing from sins an imposition of hands conferring the Spirit, in order to render explicit the positive side of the whole initiation. Perhaps in the earliest days this did not always need to be done everywhere. To this day theology says that confirmation is not absolutely necessary for salvation, implying therefore that what is given by confirmation is already in essentials conferred by baptism. It is not difficult to think it was at first only imperative to make the positive side of the initiation express and explicit in places where the outward manifestations of this gift of the Spirit (received, fundamentally speaking, in baptism itself) were not so immediately manifest as on the basis of the enthusiasm of the early Church one might have expected. It is unnecessary to overstress the fact that the apostles and not the evangelists administered confirmation in Samaria, for that is probably rather to be explained by circumstances of place and persons. Otherwise it would not be very easy to see why later on, confirmation was not kept as the exclusive privilege of the bishops.

THE CHURCH AS THE CHURCH OF THE SACRAMENTS

In such an unfolding or articulation (division would not correctly describe the reality), the early Church could have been quite convinced that it was acting according to the mind of our Lord. She was, of course, aware from Christ himself that she possessed this grace with its two aspects; that this grace was linked to membership of the Church as the fundamental sacrament of that grace; that such membership according to Christ's will was to be imparted by a rite. There we have the institution of the rite of initiation by Christ, at least, to use the modern terminology, *institutio in genere* if not *institutio in specie mutabili*. And this rite of initiation does not cease to be instituted by Christ when it is separated into two phases. There is no argument that would prove that these two phases cannot rightly be termed sacraments. Provided one does not start with the unproven assumption that the "distance" between any two sacraments must always be equal. One can see it is not so; the Church, for example, recognizes (Denzinger 907) one sacrament as *consummativum* of the sacrament of penance, and that obviously could not be said of other sacraments in relation to the sacrament of penance.

From the fact of such a partition of the complete initiation rite, which is historically at least very probable, it can be quite correctly inferred theologically, as is done in regard to other cases of the sacramental activity of the Church, that what the Church in fact did, she could legitimately do. As regards method, it is not a question, in such instances, of first laying down a very dubious *a priori* principle in advance, namely, that the Church cannot do this and that and therefore has not done it, and of then concluding that this or that cannot have happened. A more appropriate method would be to observe as impartially as possible how in fact the early Church seems to have acted, and only then infer a theological knowledge of the extent of her possibilities. That is how the theology of the sacraments has come to see in other cases that these possibilities are much greater than had previously been thought, despite the immutability of the "substance" of the sacraments.

All this is all the more relevant, because even the defined dogma that there are seven sacraments must be interpreted with a certain caution. It will probably not be disputed nowadays, that the division of holy order into several sacramental grades of order was carried out by the Church herself and not by Christ, at least as regards the division between episcopate and priesthood, supposing one does regard the episcopate as a truly separate sacramental grade of holy order. But if there are several grades of truly sacramental nature, then it is a mere matter of judging what terminology is appropriate, as to whether in the numbering of the sacraments each grade counts by itself or all the grades form only one sacrament. For in the second case one would have to admit that in order, in sharp contradistinction to the other sacraments, one is counting a *genus* and not a *species infima*. From this, however, it follows that what is essential about the definition that there are seven sacraments, is not the number, but the affirmation that the ecclesiastical rites comprised by this number are in fact of sacramental efficacy, all these and only these. Whether one then arrives at this or that number in counting the rites so designated, is in itself a matter of indifference. If one were to say there are nine sacraments, because diaconate and episcopate are sacraments too, one would not have said anything false. And if someone asserted there are only six sacraments, because he included baptism and confirmation in the one concept of initiation, as grades of this sacrament, just as the grades of order are counted as one sacrament, he would not necessarily have said anything false provided, of course, that he admitted that confirmation is a sacramental rite.

Someone might try to urge against this view that such a development of the rite of initiation certainly enriches it, perhaps more or less as the medieval rite of ordination with its *traditio instrumentorum* did, as compared with the simple imposition of hands in the early Church, but for all that "two" sacraments cannot be said to originate from it. There are two things to be said in reply. If in this development the "division" takes place so that the first "part" is regarded as sufficient for salvation and yet the second part still shares essentially in the sacramentality of the initiation as such, we have in fact two sacraments. It is not asserted that in every case the development of a rite *eo ipso* produces several sacraments, nor is it to be inferred that this is possible in no instance. Here the facts must be ascertained from experience, *a posteriori*.

This is all the more so because, as will soon be shown in more detail, it cannot be assumed as certain that what the early Church did, can always and in every case be done by the later Church, in other words that a decision of the early Church could never have absolute value and validity for all later ages, and have to be regarded as of divine law, *iuris divini*. We can therefore say that for Christ to have instituted the sacrament of confirmation, it is sufficient for him to have willed a visible form of initiation or admission to the Church, conferring on men what is essential for the Church, remission of sins and the plenitude of the Spirit. If the Church of the apostles once and for all unfolds this single initiation into two acts following one another in ritual and in time, then each act shares in the meaning and effect of the one initiation and is a sacrament. Each of the sacraments arising in this manner can be declared to have been instituted by Christ in the one initiation.

The situation is different and more puzzling in regard to the anointing of the sick referred to in the fifth chapter of St. James' epistle. There is not the slightest historical difficulty about the origin of the procedure described and recommended there. The anointing of a sick person, accompanied by prayer, is not an unusual thing that requires a special cause or origin. It is just as little surprising that such an anointing should have taken place among Christians to the accompaniment of invocation of our Lord. That in such a case health of body and forgiveness of sins should be requested together is no problem either in view of the connection between sickness and guilt in the explicit theological views of the Judeo-Christian world of that time. Why should not James have been convinced that this prayer would be heard in one way or another when made in the name of Jesus, and why should he not have expressed this conviction? It is, therefore, impossible to say that the text manifestly describes something that would be unthinkable without an express formal prescription or authorization on the part of Christ. In view of the well-founded Christian confidence in the infallible certainty of an answer to prayer, one cannot say either that the connection of the whole ritual of prayer with the conferring of grace can only be justified if founded on an express declaration of Christ, in addition to the one he gave concerning genuine prayer in faith.[3] The ritual form of this

[3] Someone who says today, "If you call on the name of the Lord contritely and ask for forgiveness of your sins, you will unfailingly receive forgiveness and grace from God", or who says, "If you ask on someone else's

prayer in which words are linked to anointing, leads a modern Catholic theologian too quickly to see it as a sacrament.

First of all, therefore, we must observe that on purely historical grounds, we are not obliged here to assume actual words of institution by Christ in order to explain the text as it stands. Someone may reply that later exegesis and the Church's teaching about the sacramentality of extreme unction prove that the text must be interpreted sacramentally, even if this cannot strictly speaking be recognized simply from its literal tenor, and that the text at least presents no obvious obstacle to such an interpretation. Now this last is true, for one can certainly conceive of Jesus' healing the sick by anointing and an actual statement of his about such anointing consequently involves no historical impossibility or patent improbability, especially when one thinks of Mark 6:13, a text the importance of which for our present question must not be exaggerated, however, for in it it is chiefly the perhaps charismatic healing of bodily illness that is prominent and no mention is made of the forgiveness of sins or of a permanent, official, not free and charismatic institution. Yet it still would remain to be asked, as we did earlier in a similar instance, how the Church recognized this possible but not inescapable reading of the text to be in fact the only correct one, when no statement of our Lord was known to her to support this later interpretation of hers. An appeal to the infallibility of the Church as the formal guarantee that in this

behalf for the forgiveness of their sins, you will infallibly be heard, provided the other person has good will, which even with a sacrament is a condition of its efficacy", they have said something that is perfectly correct, although they have not instituted a sacrament nor referred in what they have said, to such an institution by Christ.

interpretation she has not erred, is not an answer to the question how the Church recognized its truth, on what pertinent considerations and on what intrinsic principles. The confusion of these two answers is at bottom always the outcome of a tacit belief, never, of course, conscious and explicit, that infallibility involves something like a new revelation. If one does not favour this conception, which is heretical as it stands, one cannot invoke the infallibility of the Church in this question any more than it would be legitimate to answer the question how a certain person knew that Charlemagne existed, by saying that the person in question was a very learned historian. It would also have to be asked whether, even if we assume a saying of our Lord with the same content as that of James, it could be plainly recognized that it concerned a sacrament. For even on this assumption, one might ask whether the promised infallible efficacy of prayer in faith made with anointing, asserted in the supposed words of Christ, was due to the instituting of a new sacrament by Jesus. And if we are to remain in the domain of historical probability, could we imagine a clearer pronouncement in the mouth of Jesus than the one we hear from James? However one turns and twists the matter, in every case one needs in addition to the text a more general principle which makes it clear that this prayer in faith with anointing is something more than any other confident prayer in a situation of great need, which can be certain of an answer.

It must be noticed that it is the presbyters of the Church who are to recite this prayer of faith; it is therefore in some way a solemn intervention of the Church as such, the organized community. And these presbyters are "brought in". Can one say that such a prayer of faith of the Church herself, as such, in this precise critical situation in regard to salvation is, *eo ipso*, a sacrament in view of the Christ-given character of the Church, because even without any further words of institution by Christ, it cannot be anything else? If it is possible to say this and to provide sufficient grounds for the assertion from the nature of the Church and the situation that is in question, it is unnecessary to have recourse to a special pronouncement by Christ instituting this sacrament, which from the historical point of view is at the least very uncertain, yet it is possible to say with truth that our Lord instituted this sacrament because he instituted all the factors which in this case necessarily come together to form a sacrament.[4]

We must simply ask, therefore, whether there is the slightest possibility of an official prayer for God's saving help remaining unheard by God, when it is uttered by the official Church, in a situation affecting the eternal welfare of a Christian, that is, a

[4] When it is said (Denzinger 908, 926) that Christ instituted extreme unction *(instituere)*, James promulgated it *(promulgare)*, the word "promulgated" cannot simply mean the action of the apostles or evangelists reporting the special act of institution by Christ. For such a promulgation could and would have to be expressed concerning each sacrament. Clearly the Council intends here to bring out a special feature which is not found, for example, in the case of baptism. Even something of that kind points in the direction of the idea we are trying to work out here. We might notice, too, that even though the Council of Trent avoids the expression "direct", "immediate", institution, nevertheless the teaching of the Council concerning the institution of all the sacraments by Christ is interpreted by theologians in the sense that this institution was "immediate", that is, that Christ gave no one authority to institute sacraments according to their own judgment, in such a way that Christ would then have only been indirectly or mediately the cause of the sacraments. It is to be noted that the theory we are developing here does not contradict this direct and immediate institution of the sacraments, but affirms it.

person who has been made one by God in baptism and in whose regard, as a consequence, God's actual salvific will cannot be doubted; and in view of the power promised in general to prayer, previous to any question of the human being's own attitude? If this question has to be answered with a plain No (as is indeed the case, as will be shown in rather more detail in a moment), then we have a sacrament: words and rite, infallibly linked to the gift of grace. It might be thought, at first sight, that if what has been said is correct, it would follow that any prayer of the Church for a supernatural benefit would have to be a sacrament, which is obviously false. But this is not so, and

When we say that by the very fact of instituting the Church (directly of course), Christ instituted the sacraments, any intermediary able to decide the institution or non-institution of the sacraments is already excluded by that very fact. The institution of the sacraments by Christ is, therefore, an immediate one. At most it could be objected that the concrete rite as such, in which the Church performs this action in which her nature as the primal and fundamental sacrament of grace is accomplished and actualized, is not determined by Christ himself, yet this belongs to immediate institution by Christ himself. To this it may be replied that the theory does not exclude but includes Christ's having himself determined in some cases (baptism and eucharist, for example), the concrete rite too in which such a grace-giving fulfilment of the Church's nature takes place. But that does not mean he must have done so in all cases. If in some instances as the particular case requires, this is disputed or left an open question (confirmation, order, extreme unction; the case of matrimony is different again because it is not a question of a sign fixed by authority but of a natural sign), it is not the immediate institution of all the sacraments that is disputed. It is the *institutio in genere* that is being affirmed or conceded as the case may be. This latter doctrine, of course, is expounded without objection by Lugo, Arriaga, the Salmanticenses, Gonet, Billuart, the Wirceburgenses, Hurter, Billot, Van Noort, and others. See Patres S. J. Facultatum Theologicarum in Hispania Professores, *Sacrae Theologiae Summa IV* Madrid ²1953, 110f.

reflection why it is not so shows why conversely it is correct to say that this prayer of the Church in this situation for this purpose, is a sacrament.

In the first place, from the nature of the case, a sacrament is only in question when the Church's act directly concerns an individual as such, in relation to his individual salvation. That is clear. There is an *opus operatum* which is not a sacrament in this strict sense because it does not possess this characteristic: Mass as the sacrifice of the community. The act of the Church must therefore concern the individual as such in his actual supernatural situation and also concern an actual conferring of grace. This is in contrast, for example, to an indulgence, which according to many is an *opus operatum* but not a sacrament because it is forgiveness of punishment for sin and not a grant of remission of sins, grace properly so called. Furthermore the question has to be taken into account: When is the Church as such indubitably acting? When is it certain that those characteristics which belong to the Church as the eschatological presence of the triumphant grace of God are actualized absolutely and unambiguously, that is to say, when is this nature of the Church fully engaged and committed?

Negatively it can at once be said that that is not in question in every instance of an official act done by a priest at the behest of the Church or, in particular, in the case of a prayer. When a priest celebrates the liturgy for the parish in general there is no question from the start of a sacrament, in view of what has been said. And even when a prayer of the kind we have defined is spoken by the priest as such for an individual, it is not always a sacrament. Not every such prayer can be held to engage the Church as the eschatologically victorious grace in Christ. Such a prayer in very many cases, of course, will not really be requesting saving grace, and consequently there will be no unmistakable concern with God's gift of such grace on the lips of the Church in the prayer. Mostly benefits are prayed for which are of service in a person's salvation indirectly; so it is in blessings for an individual for example. But even if we suppose a priest on some order of the Church, of whatever kind, asking for grace for an individual, forgiveness of sin, for example, such an act is still not necessarily that absolute commitment in which the Church either quite unmistakably (in her eyes and God's) must manifest herself and therefore actualize her essence, or else not be the enduring sacramental presence of the unquestionable salvific will of God in Christ which has become public and irrevocable, in other words, *opus operatum*.

The Church cannot be assumed to be teaching in a way that absolutely commits her magisterium everywhere she teaches, even though she is teaching at the behest of Christ, but only when it is a special and radical case of her actualization as the presence of Christ's truth. For the same reasons, which cannot be further developed here, the same holds good of her actual realization of her nature as the presence of the grace of Christ for the individual. If such a lesser degree of actuality is possible at all, it will certainly be so when it is a question of the individual as such. For in this instance, from the very nature of the case, the Church as Church, that is, as society of the faithful and those who have been sanctified by grace (despite her mission to all individuals), is essentially less immediately engaged than when she addresses the multitude as such. For example, there is never any question of a decision of an ecclesiastical authority in an individual case as such being infallible. The reason is clear, for the

Church can only act with ultimate certainty and engage her full responsibility when it is a question of herself as such in her totality. Her infallibility is not, of course, limited to doctrine. It extends to the most varied sectors of her life, where it is not always referred to as infallibility, but amounts to the same characteristic of excluding contradiction and any absolute divergence between idea and reality, what should be done and what in fact is done. Now if her infallibility were to extend always as a matter of course to the individual case as such, the individual would inevitably, in the concrete detail of his life, leave the zone of uncertainty about his salvation and the ambiguity that belongs to the condition of a pilgrim. If we suppose him to have good will and be a member of the Church, he would share in the prerogatives of the Church herself. That, of course, is quite excluded. For the individual would pass into the divine sphere, he would really be in pure possession of grace like the Lord himself, not a recipient of redemptive grace in fear and trembling, in doubt and temptation, in the pure hope that what remains hidden is truly present.

So where the Church is dealing with the individual as such, it is to be presumed usually that she is acting without absolute certainty, or what amounts to the same thing, without absolute involvement, even when she is acting "officially". When she prays for the individual, comforts the individual, rouses his hope of salvation and so on, it is not *ipso facto* certain that here there is an instance of God's unconditional word to men. Such actions involve a certain ambiguity — is it the Church in her nature as such who is speaking, or is it men as representatives of the Church? Conversely, such an absolute involvement of the Church in her action regarding the individual as such is not thereby excluded. We already know, of course, that there are such actions. When in baptism the Church receives a human being into her realm, when she reconciles him anew to herself and to God, when she celebrates the eucharist as the highest actual fulfilment of her own being, and permits the individual to share in it[5], such actions are not merely actions of the Church, but really bring into actuality and functioning the very nature of the Church herself, her own self is involved totally and radically. Such activities share in the nature of the Church herself as the fundamental sacrament.

Can there then be a prayer of the Church which is infallibly heard, in which it is certain on the one hand that it truly answers to the nature of prayer, with the infallibility promised it by Christ, and on the other hand concerns directly an individual and his salvation as such, that is, grace for him? Is there a prayer of the Church that avoids the limiting condition that cannot usually be excluded from prayer, despite the genuine certainty of being answered which has been promised to it, the doubt, that is, whether the prayer really is in God's eyes what a prayer should be? Only the prayer of the Church as such can be of such a kind. And since not every prayer of the official Church is certainly of that kind, the prayer must occur, if there is any such prayer, in a situation that is of an essentially special kind. This can only be the situation of the person prayed for, for only in

---

[5] If the eucharist were not in the first place and essentially an act that accomplished the nature of the Church itself, but a mere action of the Church in an individual's regard, in the everyday course of his life, the reception of the eucharist, not being in such conditions a participation in the Church as such and as a whole, would not have objective certainty of effect, could not be an *opus operatum*.

this way can there be a critical situation sharply marked off from all others. Such a situation is the distress of approaching death. We do not say of the agony of death, for to view the matter for once dogmatically and purely *a posteriori,* this sacrament can be received without its being certain that the recipient is dying. But it is a matter of the distress of approaching death, though, of grave illness as the moral theologians say, words that nowadays leave the situation referred to rather vague, with its urgency, and unique quality focusing a life in its totality. James' "sickness" must indubitably be seen through the eyes of a human being of that time, with all that such a situation implied, the loneliness of helplessness, confrontation with the whole of a life now seen to be coming to its end, quite independently of the empirical question of whether it would in fact cease in the immediate future, physically speaking.

The whole person is in question, brought face to face with himself, with no more possibility of turning his mind from himself, fleeing into his job and the details of everyday life. It does not matter whether the individual human being is actually fully aware of this situation. It is there and demands to be accepted. Only someone falsely persuaded that a free person, at any moment whatsoever, can adopt any attitude he pleases quite independently of the real objective situation, not a capriciously invented one, can suppose that the personal possibilities opened out by the situation of approaching death can be coped with at will, by spontaneous asceticism, for example. The fact is that this situation is a unique one that cannot be arbitrarily constructed and in it, objectively speaking, a human being faces and is summoned to an ultimate decision, with the whole of his life in question.

Such a situation is as little susceptible as any other, concerning eternal salvation or loss as it does, of being a purely "private" concern of the Christian. If the Christian in an extremely critical situation concerning salvation and perdition, could in principle retire into a purely private individualistic domain (unless exceptionally and as a mere matter of fact), such "salvation" could have nothing to do with the Church. But if the Church as the primal sacrament of grace for the life and salvation of the individual as such, belongs to the supernatural life of the individual, this must be so above all in such a situation as this. Consequently in it the Church must be called to an action which corresponds to the unique crisis that is in question. If her own fundamentally sacramental nature can ever be involved in the circumstances of individual salvation, in certain cases if not always everywhere or arbitrarily, it must be possible here. It must be possible for her prayer to be offered here as a manifestation of the unconditional promise of salvation for the whole life of a man such as is at stake in this situation, and as a prayer that is certainly heard, because it is truly and indubitably a prayer of the Church. It must unconditionally engage the responsibility of the Church, it must radically bring into action the Church in as much as she is the fundamental sacrament of grace for the individual, as such, in critical situations, for the purpose of conferring grace on him. Therefore it is an *opus operatum* with grace as its effect. In other words it is a sacrament.

It does not, of course, follow from what has been said that one could infer all seven sacraments from the nature of the Church, by a strict deductive proof. Not does it follow that what has been said is false because such a plain and peremptory proof is simply not possible. As individual theologians we, of course, only learn from the acts proper to the Church's own life (called sacraments), and which are derived *a posteriori* from revelation, what the concrete nature of the Church is as Christ willed her to be. Complex epistemological factors are at work here which mutually condition each other, but there is no vicious circle. In the first place it must be remembered that there may be genuine abstract deductive knowledge of the nature of something, even where it is not possible without reference to the *a posteriori* experience of the individual instances actively existent and operative. For example many characteristics which Christian philosophy rightly counts as belonging to the changeless and necessary essence of man (and uses in propositions concerning the natural law), and which therefore have to be conceived as flowing of necessity from the fundamental idea of human nature, in fact would not be so deduced or recognized, if what is so deduced were not already known beforehand from actual experience. One might attempt to show, difficult as it would be, that it is necessary and essential to man, as a spiritual being endowed with a body and having a temporal life-history, who must meet other human beings in the dialogue of authentic personal relationships, to exist in two sexes, whether he wishes or not; so that his sexuality is not merely a characteristic that happens to belong to him, one that he no doubt cannot in fact abolish, but in principle a merely incidental one. It makes no difference that in fact no one presumably would undertake such an abstract deduction of sexuality as a property belonging to the essence of man, who did not already know about human sexuality as an actual fact. So too with regard to our question. We are acquainted with the sacraments; we know, because we have already experienced what they are in actual fact from their administration, that they are *de facto* acts fundamentally expressive of the Church's life, even if at first it is not clear why they are so and why other actions of the Church are not. But then in these conditions we can quite definitely recognize from the nature of the Church why they must be acts fundamentally expressive of the very essence of the Church and as a consequence possess certain characteristics such as that of the *opus operatum*.

But all this holds good of the Church herself. She experiences her own nature by fulfilling it, and, of course, what Christ expressly said about the Church belongs to that "experience", as its foundation and root. By experiencing it she perceives the different levels of her activities by the extent to which she is implicated in them. And so she can recognize that certain acts flowing from her nature are fundamentally and unconditionally the accomplishment of that nature and so are what we call sacraments. The Church could not know this, and certainly the individual theologian could not, if this nature or essence were only given in an abstract idea and not in its real fulfilment in activity; the Church could not abstractly deduce the sacraments, and especially their sevenfold number, from that idea alone. But possessing and recognizing her essence in its concrete fulfilment, she can understand that such and such definite activities which she has already carried out spontaneously in accordance with what she is – always a condition of self-analysis – are essential to her own nature, without really having to be informed of this again explicitly. It makes little sense to object that after all it would be possible to think of and construct other such acts, and so deduce more than seven sacraments. In the first place that is not at all easy to do convincingly, even theoretically as an experiment. Consequently one might calmly wait for the as yet untried attempt to be made, and if it were, one could then show in all probability that these imagined additional acts in which the essence of the Church found expression cannot really be unmistakably proved to be of equal rank with the seven sacraments that do exist.

Furthermore it would have to be pointed out that such acts, perhaps abstractly possible in themselves, are not in fact performed by her, so that there are in fact no more sacraments. A radical self-commitment without awareness of it, is, of course, impossible, and the Church by her affirmation that there are seven sacraments and no more, declares such an awareness to be not present even in an implicit form, and expressly excludes it. Then too it would have to be said that if such supplementary acts realizing and bringing into activity the very essence of the Church are not forthcoming, even after the Church has already attained the full actual accomplishment of her nature, the reason for this can only be that such additional fundamental activities are not possible, for otherwise they would already have been performed and manifested. This can be asserted even more readily as a matter of course, if one assumes, as one may, that in certain circumstances there could be an irreversible historical decision of the Church which by the nature of the case is to be regarded as *iuris divini*, even if before the decision was taken it was not absolutely inevitably necessary for it to be taken. Once made, however, it is irrevocable, because it derives from the divinely ordained essence of the Church. If one considers that conceivable in principle, one is still left with the possibility of maintaining the sevenfold number of the sacraments as *iuris divini*, without thereby prejudging the question whether it would not have been possible, when the Church was still at the stage of formation, for her one fundamentally sacramental essence to have unfolded in an even larger number of such basic acts expressive of her nature.

It has already been indicated that such a fact must almost inescapably be reckoned with, in at least one instance, that of holy order. It is open to any Catholic theologian to regard diaconate, priesthood and episcopate as the articulation or distribution of her one power of order derived from Christ. This is all the more so because all the great theologians of the Middle Ages conceived the lower grades of order as sacramental, and it is even now permissible to consider that they were then true sacraments, even if one wants to maintain that they are so no longer. This opinion is indeed more probable, for reasons which cannot be gone into here, but which follow from the principles we have enunciated. If one counts all the sacraments according to their *species infima* and not according to the wider *genus,* one can even today count nine sacraments, on account of the three parts of order. And one can say that this number is not and was not an absolutely necessary one. This could be said by someone who wants to hold in an intelligible manner that the Church today can no longer abolish these three grades of order because they were formed in that early Church which must be looked on in a strict theological sense as the Church still in process of being constituted in existence. Then that historical decision must almost inevitably be regarded as irreversible in the way mentioned above. It was freely made, it would appear, as we can see from the way the apostles introduced the diaconate, nevertheless cannot be abolished, as must be held by anyone for whom these three grades of order are *iuris divini* and unalterable.

In this section we have been concerned with the question whether the problem of the historical difficulty of proving the institution by Christ of certain sacraments could not be given a better and easier solution if approached from the standpoint of the Church as the primal sacrament, with certain fundamental and essential acts in which her nature finds actualization, as the sacraments. The reflections showed first of all why such a question needs to be propounded anew in more acute form; historically explicit words of institution are not only not historically available, but are demonstrably improbable on historical grounds. These reflections were fully worked out on the positive side as regards extreme unction, but partly postponed to later sections of the inquiry in the cases of matrimony and order. In regard to confirmation the matter was brought, it seems to us, to a positive conclusion.

In fact traditional theology has already taught from other angles and with other concepts, the basic principle which we took as starting-point. It affirmed that in the New Testament in contrast to the old covenant, there are no signs of grace prescribed by Christ himself (we would say which Christ established with the Church, as the essential acts proper to her, whereby her nature is accomplished) which are not also true sacraments. This traditional theology then demonstrated, for example, the sacramentality of marriage precisely from this general axiom. So, for example, we find in Pesch (*Praelectiones dogmaticae* VI Prop. IX): *Omne signum quod in nova lege ex praecepto Dei hominibus applicandum est ad significandum gratiae est etiam efficax ad producendam gratiam.* For Pesch, therefore, the rites effected by the Church, which manifest God's saving action in regard to men, are necessarily efficacious causes of this grace, that is, *opus operatum,* when they are instituted as such by God and not merely determined by the Church's good pleasure. From this thesis it is not far to the theory we have been expounding here. It is only necessary to assume in addition that the indispensable prescription by God and Christ of this manifestation of grace in symbolic forms took place by being implied by the founding of the Church. Such a supposition cannot, however, have involved any insuperable difficulty for Pesch either, because he used the axiom we have quoted, and which is proved from the difference between the old covenant and the new, to show the sacramentality of marriage, without requiring a demonstration that the institution of the sign by Christ took place by an explicit declaration.[6]

f. Sacramental and personal piety

If we view the sacraments as acts in which the Church accomplishes her nature as the sign of the eschatological presence of God's grace in Christ, we can also understand more easily how in the process of sanctification of the individual, sacramental event and personal event penetrate and mutually presuppose each other, without coinciding completely. For we find the same relation in doctrine about the Church in general, between visible membership of the Church on the one hand, and on the other, the interior bond of grace linking the individual with the Spirit of the Church through personal faith and love. It would, therefore, only be necessary to show in the treatise on the Church in general what the relation is between the Church as a visible society and the Church as an interior community of faith and grace, for all the essentials to have been said about the relation, difference, and

[6] See Ch. Pesch, *Praelectiones dogmaticae* VII Prop. LIII n. 702 ed. V (Freiburg 1920).

mutual connection between sacraments as rites of the visible historical society and the personal acceptance in faith of interior grace through, under and by this ritual act, in other words, between sacramental and personal piety. We must, however, refer the reader to our earlier treatment of this question.[7]

We shall note later what follows from the principle developed here in regard to the sacramental character.

[7] See K. Rahner, *Schriften zur Theologie* II (Einsiedeln ³1958) pages 115—141.

II

THE VARIOUS SACRAMENTS AS ACTS IN WHICH THE CHURCH'S NATURE IS FULFILLED

THE ECCLESIOLOGICAL ASPECT OF THE SACRAMENTS AS EVENTS IN THE INDIVIDUAL'S SANCTIFICATION

1. *General Considerations*

WE HAVE already said that the Church is not a mere institute for eternal welfare, administering powers that God happened to entrust to her, but which he might just as well have given to another to administer. Since the Church herself is the sign of the presence of the grace of God in the world, because Christ continues his presence in history through her, the Church is not an offer of God to the world of such a kind that it remains in doubt whether it will be accepted or not; it is rather the sign of present and victorious grace. Acceptance itself, however, can only take place in the individual, for victorious grace is only present where the subjective holiness of an individual is achieved through it. (The infusion of grace at the baptism of an infant without such acceptance in faith and works, can be left out of account here. In the first place the Church cannot primarily consist of infants; the purely objective nature of their Christianity prevents their being typical Christians. Furthermore such a grace given solely through the sacrament without the intervention of personal decision as a supernatural habitus of the theological virtues is entirely intended for personal use by the recipient, and only in that way attains the full perfection of its nature, because grace is ultimately a sharing in the actual plenitude of God's life and all merely habitual grace is only rightly to be understood as the ontological presupposition of that life.) Consequently the Church as historical sign of victorious grace only attains the highest actualization of her own nature when grace is victorious in this sense in the individual and also is tangibly expressed and really occurs for the individual's sanctification. That is exactly what happens in the sacraments.[1] This is what has now to be considered in each of the sacraments, and all along it is a matter of seeing that the sacraments, precisely as events in the spiritual life and sanctification of the individual, have an ecclesiological aspect. For it goes without saying that this aspect belongs to the sacraments as official acts of the Church who dispenses the mysteries of God.

Before we go on to consider the sacraments from this angle, another general observation might be made. It is profitable to reflect on the question why Jesus, according to the testimony of the gospels, instituted and spoke about the various sacraments

[1] It is true that from that point of view, a closer examination would show that the Church as Church which attains the highest degree of actuality in administering the sacraments, and the Church which is truly holy in her members and is manifestly holy, is necessarily one and the same Church. These two factors condition one another in her, although it cannot be absolutely certain that they coincide, if the Church is also to be the Church of those who are still pilgrims in hope, and who must work out their salvation in view of a judgment of God which has not yet been made known.

in such an apparently unsystematic and haphazard way. There is no mention in his life of several of them: confirmation, extreme unction, matrimony, order (as a sacrament). The others are referred to almost incidentally, without method and system. Penance is mentioned first (Matt. 16 and 18), unless we are to assume that baptism is first spoken about, on account of the baptism of John and because of John, chapter three. It is even possible to say that Jesus was not concerned at all about systematic arrangement, that he did not envisage under so abstract a concept as sacrament the tangible salvific acts of his love in the individual's regard in their concrete reality. But if once again we envisage the Church as the fundamental sacrament, we shall perhaps achieve an even better understanding of this striking fact. When the Church is considered in her hierarchical order as the community of redemption in Christ, in contrast to the people of the covenant of the old testament, attention will turn less to the question by what rite one enters it, than to the fact that by reason of its hierarchical constitution full membership is always subject to the control of those who in this sense can bind and loose.[2] And with that we have already got what nowadays we call the sacrament of penance. When this new community of those who believe in Jesus Christ separates itself more and more from the world which thrust out the Lord of that community,

---

[2] This is all the more so because when the entry of an individual into Christ's sacred community was in question, thoughts must have been much more occupied with belief in Christ, acceptance of the *basileia* (kingdom, rule) of God that was being manifested in him, through the *metanoia* (conversion) of the whole man, than with the particular rite of such admission to membership. There is no reason for objecting that the same must apply to penance of the individual within the community, that is

and consequently his followers, into death, we see the moment when this community grasps her own innermost nature, in the ritual celebration of that death which is her true life. That is the eucharist. It is obvious that this highest accomplishment and fulfilment by the community of its own nature, in its essence and totality, must be celebrated by the authoritative act of those whom Christ has appointed as leaders of this sacred community. It is then scarcely necessary to state that the transmission of this authority, constitutive as it is of the Church, is a sacrament, the sacrament of holy order. For it is willed by Christ, and it is a fundamental act of the Church herself who maintains her own historical existence by such an historically manifest and tangible action. When Christ gave the apostles his authority and knew and stated himself to be the redeemer of all and as the end and purpose of history, as the judge who is to come, he had already

to say, that in this case too attention must involuntarily have turned first of all to the personal, "subjective" change of heart and not to the sacramental rite. The objection is not pertinent, for the situation is quite different from that of a man's first conversion. One who belongs to Jesus' sacred community, who has been admitted into Christ's kingdom of God, which is at hand, must live in holiness. If he sins, therefore, he offends against the whole status which he accepted in his new existence, and against the Church. Consequently in such a case his attention must inevitably at once turn to the contradiction between his sin and Jesus' community. What then must at once be described is not the "rite" of a renewed forgiveness of sins (as such) dispensed by the Church but the correct manner in which the holy community reacts to the sin of its member. This reaction, when it is "loosing" not "binding" is in fact a sacrament, but is not looked upon as baptism is, as a symbolical rite, but as a judicial act of passing judgment (as a *krisis:* 1 Cor. 5:3-12; 2 Cor. 2:6f.). As of course dogmatic theology rightly says down to the present day, with the Council of Trent, the "form" of the sacramental sign in penance consists in a judicial act of the Church. It is something that is quite different in nature from symbolic affirmed his Church to be final and irrevocable, and in a milieu familiar with the conferring and the handing on of office by the ritual imposition of hands, he had already said all that there was to be said about ritual transmission of ministry. That such a rite was also a sacrament will have to be shown later.

Then almost incidentally it can be stated how the rite is to take place which will first admit someone outside into that community, which until then had concentrated more on its own inner life. That would give us baptism. Only when the Church at Pentecost experiences herself to be the Church of the Spirit, endowed with the charismata, will she explicitly advert to the fact that the full rite of admission must comprise ablution of guilt and the imposition of hands for the reception of the Spirit: confirmation will be seen explicitly as a fundamental act proper to the Church which necessarily expresses her own nature in the constitution of a full citizen. That is to say, confirmation is

ritual gesture. Such small observations show what an impediment it can be to a knowledge of the precise nature of the various sacraments if their actual place in real life is passed over and they are envisaged more or less abstractly in terms of the general schema or type of a "sacrament as such". In that way many insights that are important for the pastoral administration of the sacraments become harder to attain than they need be. Perhaps, too, dialogue with Protestant theologians about controverted points of theology in regard to the number of the sacraments might be carried on with better chance of agreement if the number seven were not put at the beginning, as is commonly done in our dogmatic treatises, but was considered as a relatively subordinate consequence, which is only arrived at the end, after a calm consideration in the light of Scripture of all the individual events and activities there are in the Church, as Scripture testifies, and the nature of which can be grasped before they are subsumed under the generic concept of sacrament, the number seven being reached at that point.

a sacrament.[3] Later still the gaze of faith will be able to see that marriage, because of its character, indicated in Scripture, as type or symbol of God's love in Christ for men; of the love that brings about the new and eternal testament, must be in the Church, for the Church and for mankind, a sign of the grace of God which cannot be thought of as absent from Christian living. It is a sign that therefore belongs to the basic manifestations of Christian life, and because it is such a fundamental sign of grace in the Church, cannot be an empty sign but in the way proper to it, is a sacrament too.

It is not very difficult to understand, if we open ourselves to the Church's sense of her faith, that the Church must be at a pitch of highest actuality in her own nature when she assures an individual human being that he belongs to her not to the world, when in his mortal distress he is threatened with the loss of this world in good or ill. And with that we have the sacramentality of the prayer in faith with anointing, which we call extreme unction, without our necessarily having to postulate an explicit statement by Jesus to his apostles.

But the same *proviso* must be made in regard to these discussions which we have already expressly made earlier. Deductions of this kind are made with the concrete nature of the Church in view before our eyes. They are attempts to imitate and recapture insights in the Church's awareness of her own faith which she attained in the course of a long history guided by the Spirit, not

---

[3] These considerations are not intended to suggest that Jesus made no explicit statements about the sacraments. Our point is that we need not depend upon them as much as positivist theologians sometimes seem to think. They tend to be embarrassed when such statements cannot be discovered and, in their dilemma, postulate these somewhat too confidently.

absolutely self-supporting, independent, mathematical proofs. This brings us to the actual theme of this second part of our inquiry, the ecclesiological aspect of the various sacraments, not so much as official actions of the Church administering them, but as events in the individual spiritual life and sanctification of their recipient.

2. The Eucharist

We begin not with baptism, as the usual treatises on the sacraments do, but with the eucharist. It cannot simply be put on a level with the other sacraments and listed along with them. The Council of Trent points that out (Denzinger 846, 876). It follows from the real presence of the Body of Christ; from the fact that here there is not only a sacrament but also the sacrifice of the new covenant; from the teaching that sees the eucharist as the source of the other sacraments.[4] Indubitably the celebration of the eucharist is an absolutely central event in the Church. Even nowadays it needs repeatedly to be stressed that mass should not be viewed by the faithful (the danger is far from remote), as merely the production of Christ's real presence in the sacrament for the purpose of communion regarded in an extremely individualistic way. Such an idea is unacceptable, though not because the point of view of a personal, individual meeting with the "bridegroom of the soul" is false or to be disparaged, and it is not right that it should be attacked by those who want to manage without a personal spiritual life. The individualistic

---

[4] See M. de la Taille, *Mysterium fidei* (Paris 1931).

narrowness must not be tolerated because it mutilates the faith, if not in theory, at least in practice. For faith tells us that the mass is so much the sacrifice of the Church, that even a priest's most private mass is always the Church's sacrifice, and as far as possibility allows, must appear as such (Denzinger 944, 945). Communion is a deeper incorporation into the mystical Body of Christ, because the redeemer has left his real Body to his Church, through which he wished to have all Christians joined together (Denzinger 873a, 875).

We can and must say that participation in the physical Body of Christ by the reception of this sacrament imparts the grace of Christ to us in so far as this partaking of one bread (1 Cor. 10:14–8) is an efficacious sign of the renewed, deeper, and personally ratified participation and incorporation in that Body of Christ in which one can share in his Holy Spirit, that is to say, the Church. In other words *res et sacramentum*, first effect and intermediary cause of the other effects in this sacrament is the more profound incorporation into the unity of the Body of Christ. In support of this we might recall the passage from St. Paul quoted above, the first eucharistic prayers in the *Didache*, the eucharistic teaching of St. Augustine, who always makes this aspect so prominent that he could be suspected of an overspiritual volatilization of the doctrine of the real presence. Indications are found in St. Thomas, who regards the eucharist as the sacrament of the Church's unity (III q. 82 a. 2 ad 2). If someone prefers to call the Body of Christ itself present under the species and becoming a sacramental sign for us through them, the *res et sacramentum* and the unity of symbol formed by species and words as *sacramentum tantum*, with all the supernatural effects in grace thought of as the *res*, which is certainly the usual view (Denzinger 415), he will at least have to say that the Body of Christ is a sign of his grace, by its being in possession of the Church as a sign of her own unity, pledge of eternal life and as sacrificial offering to God. He would also have to arrange among themselves in intelligible order the various effects of the eucharist, which he comprises under the concept of *res sacramenti*. Then however, once again, union with the mystical Body of Christ whose life is the Spirit, by analogy with the other sacraments especially baptism from which the idea of *sacramentum* and *res* originally came, would still be the effect of the sacrament that is prior to all others. So it is that Innocent III in the passage just quoted only brings out *unitas* and *caritas* as the effect of the sacrament. He is still thinking quite entirely in terms of the Church (Denzinger 415).

It must further be borne in mind that the words of consecration even when physically they are past, always belong to the sacramental sign as present. Now this form of words speaks of the new and eternal covenant that was concluded in the Blood of Christ. Christ is present in the sacrament under these words. (It is not a question here whether they always require to be recited explicitly or not for consecration to be valid.) He is therefore present as bond of unity, as the foundation of the covenant between God and men, as the Church's unity therefore. Because he really gives himself in ever new sacramental manifestation as sacrifice for the Church (Eph. 5:25 f.) and as sacrifice of the Church, because he exists in the Church in visible and tangible sacramental form, there *is* the Church. She is most manifest and in the most intensive form, she attains the highest actuality of her own nature, when she celebrates the eucharist. For here everything that goes to form the Church is found fully and manifestly present: her separation from the world (even today this demands and justifies a sort of discipline of the secret, *disciplina arcani*[5]); her hierarchical structure (priest and people); her attitude of dutiful receptivity to God, which forbids her to be an end in herself (sacrifice); her recitation of the efficacious words which render present what they proclaim (the *anamnesis*, the words of commemoration, are the primal constitutive words of the Church[6]); her unity (the one bread of which all eat in the sacred meal which unites all who take part in it); her expectation of the final kingdom, the glory of which is ritually anticipated in this celebration; her penitential spirit in offering the sacrifice which was offered for the sin of the world: Denzinger 875, 940: *donum paenitentiae concedens;* the invincibility of the grace of God, which was definitively given her, that she might be holy, for she has him who is the final victory and she already celebrates in advance the ultimate victory of God's kingdom, by proclaiming the death of the Lord, who is the victory, in the consciousness that she will do that until he comes again (1 Cor. II:26); her profound readiness to serve others (the sacrifice to God *pro totius mundi salute*).

In connection with this it would be possible to indicate much else that can only be alluded to rather as inquiry than as statement. It has already been briefly remarked upon that the eucharist is really the starting-point of all kerygmatic, apostolic preaching in the Church. The *anamnesis*, the words of commemoration are the very central words of the Church because in the most

---

[5] See K. Rahner, *Sendung und Gnade* (Innsbruck 1959).
[6] See K. Rahner, *Schriften zur Theologie* III (Einsiedeln ³1959), IV (Einsiedeln 1960).

real and intensive way they make present for our salvation what they signify. For that reason all other words in the Church are ultimately only preparation, exposition and defence of these words alone, in which the incarnate Word of God comes into our space and time as our salvation. Furthermore we should have to consider in what way the Church in general, the whole Church, is given with and in the single congregation or parish, by whose celebration she is rendered present as a totality in her highest degree of actuality. For it will not represent the state of affairs to which we are referring with any precision if we view the single congregation simply as a segment of the Church, comparable to an administrative district in a State, nor if the Church as a whole is hypostatized and regarded purely juridically as the subject of the celebration of mass in the individual parish.[7] On the basis of the preceding considerations regarding the historical presence of redemptive grace, it seems possible to gain some insight that where the eschatologically triumphant grace of God is present in historically tangible form, however this happens or whoever the human subject involved may be, the Church as the consecrated and socially organized people of God is manifested, and so the total Church is present. From this one could perhaps approach the Pauline conception of the Church as a whole and as individual congregation in their mutual relationship, just as in time of Christ individual groups and fraternities thought of their relation to the whole people of the covenant, from which they were distinct and of which they nevertheless felt they were representative as mediators of its promises.

[7] On this see: K. Rahner, *Zur Theologie der Pfarre*, in Hugo Rahner, *Die Pfarre* (Freiburg 1956) 27-39; K. Rahner, *Primat und Episkopat*, in: K. Rahner, *Sendung und Gnade* (Innsbruck 1959) 247-254.

In all these reflections it must never be overlooked that holy communion has this reference to the Church, even as an event in the individual's sanctification. It is the Church that gives the individual the Body of Christ, which she has in her possession as the pledge of her redemption and the presence of grace in her, and she makes the individual share, for his sanctification, in the unity, love and plenitude of the Spirit of this holy community of God's covenant, and so she fills him with all grace. Only a person who is prepared in principle to entrust himself to the whole activity of the Church that takes place in the eucharist, through which she is more consecrated to God, given over more profoundly to the death of Christ, becomes more closely one, approaches more and more the consummation of all things in the coming of the Lord, will share even in the blessings and graces of this sacrament for the individual. For ultimately these are nothing but that deeper and deeper union with the Church, her action and her lot.

3. Baptism

Little need be said about baptism, not because its ecclesiological aspect would be hard to discover, but because it is everywhere expressly stated and obvious. As is well known, baptism according to the formal teaching of the Church (Denzinger 324, 570a, 696, 864, 1413, 1936a; Cod. Iur. Can. c. 87) is at least the sacrament of incorporation into the Church. But we can go further. This incorporation, as adherence in faith to the sacred community of the Lord, in which the *protestatio fidei* is from the first not the enunciation of an individual and private view of the world, but the proclamation of acceptance of the Church's belief, adherence to a belief already there and manifestly exercised in the Church, is not only one effect in fact of baptism, but is itself a sacrament, a sign of the other effects of the grace of baptism. To be incorporated into the Church is, therefore *sacramentum et res* in this sacrament of Christian initiation. That full membership of the Church as the Body of Christ vivified by the Spirit, provided no obstacle is put in the way of the influence of the Spirit of the Church, can bring with it all the other effects of baptism, so that this membership can therefore be regarded as *sacramentum et res,* needs no lengthy proof after what we have said about the nature of the Church. It should also be remembered that in the old testament and in the new, the subject of redemption to which God's mercy is addressed is in the first place always the people, the nations, the Church as the partner in the covenant (which the individual as such cannot be), and the individual only shares in grace as a member of such a people of the promise.

Now it has become customary to consider the sacramental "character" as the first effect of baptism and as the mediating cause of the other effects and so as *sacramentum et res* in regard to them. What we have said should not and need not be understood as in contradiction to this common teaching. By character, something concrete must be signified. One must ask what this *signum spirituale et indelibile* (Denzinger 852), which is impressed on the soul really means and in actual fact is. If one avoids arbitrary mystification about this sign, and bears in mind the origin of the doctrine of baptismal character in Augustine[8], it

---

[8] It is derived with him entirely from the knowledge that baptism cannot be repeated and from no other theological sources, so that it is possible to say what follows from that about the character. It is always for Augustine

will be quite possible to say that the import of the character is the Church of Christ's express and enduring claim to the baptized person, produced by a sacramental and historical event. It is, then, unimportant for our purpose whether the character is said to be identical with this condition of being claimed by the Church or that this being in duty bound to the Church is founded on an ontological state of the soul given at baptism. For if one goes on to ask in what this ontological state of the soul consists, what its meaning and function is, and if one does not arbitrarily, without examination and without reference back to the original sources, fill the formal breadth and vacuity of such a concept (ontological state, physical quality, etc.), with some conceptual scheme of one's own choosing, one cannot but come across this claim of the Church on an individual which has been expressed visibly and tangibly in time and place and therefore is a permanent one. If one does not, it is only by very artificial elaborate explanations that one can show how the character is a "sign". For if one wants to answer that question without such devices, one must point to an element that is "perceptible"[9], for without it there is no sign, and one that is lasting, even though deriving from an action, for otherwise there would be no *signum indelibile*. What could one point to except what we have described? As a fact having social duration, it is not visible like a house, for example, but it has a really historical

---

a sign of belonging to Christ's flock and militia, even when, by reason of the baptism of heretics and schismatics, the sheep may have fled and the soldier deserted.

[9] It is, to put it mildly, absurd, to say that this sign is a sign for God and the angels, simply so as to be able to maintain that it is still a sign even when it is a completely invisible reality.

and social perceptibility, just as the possession of an office which, constituted by a visible transmission, itself is concretely tangible and manifest. The teaching of St. Thomas on baptismal character does not necessarily contradict this view. It is sufficient to ask why through the baptismal character a human being shares in the priesthood of Christ and how this participation can be distinguished from the one that derives from grace. The answer must surely be that it belongs to a man in as much as he is a member of the Church and remains in relation to the Church; because the Church as the visible Church in the world of space and time (not only in the depth of the conscience sanctified by grace) continues the priestly function of Christ the high-priest.

In order not to misunderstand what has been said, it must always be remembered that even where a baptized person is no longer, as the encyclical *Mystici corporis* has it, in the full sense a member of the Church because he is a heretic or a schismatic, he always remains in relation to the Church through the enduring fact of having been baptized; and this does not belong in the same way to an unbaptized person, even if he is justified.

4. Confirmation

It is not difficult to perceive an ecclesiological aspect in confirmation either. If we reflect on what the Acts of the Apostles says about confirmation, it is clear that the Spirit conferred by the imposition of hands in this sacrament is always regarded as a Spirit that manifests itself externally in the charismata. Because the Spirit was not recognized at baptism alone, it was said at that time that the Holy Spirit had not yet been received. The Spirit that had not been received was the Spirit whose mighty sway and influence had not yet been experienced. That too had to be given. It did not necessarily have to take place in a way we today probably would think of as "charismatic", externally remarkable, and miraculous. For we see in the first epistle to the Corinthians that Paul on occasion counts quite unexciting gifts and talents among the charismata which the Spirit of God gives to individual Christians and members of the Church for the good of the whole Church.

What is in question here is as follows. The grace of God has a double direction or movement. It is the grace of dying with Christ, a grace of the cross, of the downfall of the world, of being taken out of the aeon of the law, death, sin and also of all aims and purposes that belong to this world alone. All that is expressed in baptism as a descent into death with Christ; it takes place by being represented in sign. But at the same time the grace of Christ is the grace of incarnation, a grace of acceptance of the world for its transfiguration, a grace the victory of which will be visible in the world, in its healing, preservation, redemption from the nothingness to which it is subject, and such a grace is also one of mission to the world, work in the world, world-transformation. The particular function of the grace that is given more particularly to the individual as his special task, is decided by God's vocation and by the distribution of the charismata of the Spirit, which are nothing but the special directions in which one and the same Spirit unfolds its action. All receive it and with it all can and are to serve, even those who apparently have received the opposite grace. And because the second direction or tendency of the one grace of Christ, incarnate, crucified, and risen, is just as essential as the first, which is that of death with Christ, it must be expressed in a sacramental rite of its own, although in a certain sense it is only a question in this sacrament of the same grace as in baptism becoming visibly apparent and manifest in history. This grace only "appears" under another aspect, and, of course, thereby, as through all sacramental manifestation, becomes deeper and increases. This second sacrament is confirmation, imposition of hands to receive the charismatic Spirit of a world-transforming mission in the accomplishment of the task proper to the Church as such, for she as holy Church, in the plenitude of her vitality and transfiguring power, is to be God's witness in the world that he does not abandon the whole mundane creation to its sinful nothingness, but redeems, preserves and transfigures it.

When we call confirmation the sacrament of strength in the faith and in professing the faith before the world, this must not be taken to mean only that the Christian receives in confirmation the grace of the Holy Spirit to keep his faith, to save it, but with great trouble, in a world hostile to it. The comprehensive sense is intended which we have indicated. It is in this light that the apostolate must be viewed, on which the Christian who is made an adult by confirmation, is sent. It is not so much ultimately an apostolate of defence and self-affirmation of the Church, as a mission to the task which the Church has been given, not to assert herself anxiously and save herself, but in order that the world should be saved through her. The task imposed on the Christian by confirmation is therefore the obligation of an apostolic mission into the world itself, as a part of the function and task of the Church to transform it and bring it into the kingdom of God which is at hand. It is not so much the grace of individual care for the salvation of one's own soul as the charismatic gift, that is, one rich in blessing for others, of collaborating in the mission of the Church, using all the gifts which may be of service to the salvation of all.

5. Penance

That the sacrament of penance[10] has an ecclesiological aspect requires no lengthy explanation. If with the whole of tradition down to the thirteenth century and in accordance with correct exegesis of the relevant texts, we give the words of Matthew chapters sixteen and eighteen about "binding and loosing" their full value, we have a reference to what we nowadays call the sacrament of penance. These passages concern the way Christ's holy community is to deal with a sinful member. If such a member of that sacred society which by her life is to announce the victory of grace and the coming of the kingdom of God sins contumaciously, grievously, this cannot be a matter of indifference to Christ's Church, for otherwise, of course, she would belie her nature. She must react against such a sin, through which the member of the community not only puts himself in contradiction to God but also to the Church of Christ, for the Church in her members and by their holiness must be the primal sacramental sign of the victorious grace of God. For that reason the Church "binds" this sinner, that is, she draws away from him "on earth" by some form of exclusion, not to be confused with excommunication as it is at present, but similar, for example, to the present-day exclusion from holy communion

---

[10] See K. Rahner, Bußsakrament, in: *Lexikon f. Theologie u. Kirche* II (Freiburg ²1958) 826–838.

with the obligation of confession. The consequence is that the sinner is no longer regarded by God as belonging to that holy community and for that reason cannot share in the grace which is acknowledged by God in men to the degree in which they are members of the Church of Christ. If on the contrary the Church raises the ban "on earth and in heaven", she "looses" him on earth, through a renewed and full recognition of his reconciliation with the Church; to the extent, we may say, that this has a sacramentally symbolic value, the sinner is "loosed" in heaven too. God effectively regards him in the full sense as a member of that community which the Son has gathered on earth for heaven, as those who are his, the beloved of his Father, those who will possess the kingdom. And in that and by that God forgives him his sins.

From this it is at once clear that sin itself has an ecclesiological aspect. Reconciliation through the Church is also reconciliation with the Church. The *pax cum ecclesia* is *sacramentum et res* of reconciliation with God.

The ecclesiological aspect of the sacrament of penance becomes deeper and more extensive if we recall the Thomistic doctrine that the acts of the contrite penitent confessing to the Church are part of the sacramental sign itself. For that means that the contrite sinner and the Church together make up the sign in which in the public, social, historical domain of the Church (which is not necessarily *in foro externo*), both the act of the human being as a baptized member of the Church, and the reconciling act of God in the human being's regard, all attain visible and manifest expression. What happens here in the sacrament of penance is an actualization of the Church's own essence. She is manifested in the penitent himself (who co-operates in her liturgy), as the penitent Church of sinners ever bathing the feet of Christ with her tears and hearing his words, "Neither will I condemn thee". It is the Church's very nature in act, in as much as she, holy Church, withdraws in judgment from sin, (hearing the confession, judicial verdict, imposition of a penance), and so lifts again the darkness cast by her rejection of sin, the sin of one of her members. It is a vital expression of the Church's essence, as bearer of God's grace-giving words, which she addresses here to the individual and so effectually fulfils her own nature as the abiding sacrament of God's mercy in the world.

Thus in this sacrament again and again the Church's action manifests that the Church herself in the unity of her judicial holiness and of her ever renewed mercy to the sinner, is the indestructible sign of the grace of God that is irrevocably given in the world as long as this aeon lasts. Because there is this irrevocable grace of God, holding sin within its mercy during this epoch of the world, and because this grace has its historical presence in the Church, there is within the Church in regard to members of the Church herself a sacrament of the unconquerable readiness of God to forgive, the sacrament of penance. In the common action of the priest as the authorized spokesman of the Church, and of the penitent human being, the fundamental nature of the Church herself is manifested.

6. Holy Order

Before we can go on to examine the ecclesiological aspect of the sacrament of holy order considered as an event that sanctifies an individual, there remains a task to be completed which was left unfinished earlier. We indicated that with this sacrament, as with some others, words of institution uttered by Christ are not in all historical probability to be reckoned on, words that in this particular case would not only explicitly express the authority to transmit office and ministry but would also expressly affirm the sacramental nature of this transmission. We have not yet, however, explained how the sacramentality of this transmission of ministry in the Church follows from the principle that the Church is the primal and fundamental sacrament.

We can start with that basic axiom. When in respect to an individual, in situations decisive for his salvation, the Church accomplishes one of the actions proper to her, engaging her responsibility fully, and actualizing her essence as the primal sacrament of grace, there we have a sacrament. Consequently the existence of the sacrament has its ground in the existence of the Church as primal sacrament, and when no express words of institution have been handed down to us, the establishment of the Church by Christ can be regarded as the institution of such an action and therefore of a sacrament. The recognition by the Church of her own nature as she fulfils it in this way, can be the gnoseological ground for her recognition of the sacramentality of a sacrament. And as the Church is never without this means of recognizing a particular sacrament, and her reflection on her own intrinsic nature lasts through history, there is no need to postulate that the explicit recognition of the sacramentality of such an actuation of her essence (which we call a sacrament), must always have been present or else, without a new revelation, be lacking in any legitimate source or origin.

The question we have to propound and answer in greater detail is a double one. Why is the handing on of spiritual power in the Church a fundamental action for her, radically involving her own very nature? And why is the end and purpose of this act not the office and ministry itself, but also, and necessarily, a special grace of state which sanctifies the bearer of the office? These two questions are to be distinguished. Not every fundamental action of the Church is, as such, a sacrament. An infallible definition is such an action in which the Church's very nature, but in another direction, is involved, yet it is not a sacrament. Conversely an act of the Church, for example, a prayer in the ordinary course of the liturgy or in a sacramental, can have as its purpose a grace and yet not be a sacrament in the strict sense. We have the same thing when a Christian says something convincing to another in his personal circumstances which awakens his faith and trust in forgiveness; it is quite possible to regard this in a true sense not as the words of a "private individual" but as the words of the Church too; for, of course, they can be spoken by a baptized and confirmed Christian, or by a teacher authorized by the Church, or by parents in a sacramental marriage, valid in the eyes of the Church and symbolizing the Church. The two questions must not, accordingly, be confused, although we shall see in any case that both can be answered from a proper understanding of the Church.

A positive answer to the first is not far to seek. The really fundamental offices in the Church are the most indispensable constituents of the Church herself. She only exists by possessing and transmitting the functions given her by Christ, and the powers bound up with and serving them. By the transmission of office, especially when this gives power to exercise the fundamental functions of the Church, to bear witness to Christ's message, to celebrate the eucharist, and, we must add, conversely, to hand on these powers which are constitutive of the Church, the Church in one important respect keeps on re-constituting herself anew. So that is quite definitely an indispensable fundamental function of the Church, provided the Church is not thought to spring into existence afresh perpetually in an ever actual charismatic beginning but is recognized to have both an historically visible and tangible form and likewise an historically manifest temporal continuity. And this is in fact the case. For historical form and temporal continuity are not to be separated in a reality that has existence in time. And the idea of succession is directly present and discernible in the New Testament and in the world of that time.

Why, however, is this fundamental act of the Church handing on her ministry and by so doing constituting herself anew, an act which also has as its purpose, the sanctification of the man who receives the ministry, and so merits the name of sacrament? Here too the answer is to be sought in the nature of the Church. This shows that it is not a matter of indifference to the meaning and nature of ministry in the Church whether it is exercised and administered with holiness or not. To be sure the ministry keeps its validity and its bearer his authority and power, even if as an individual he is a sinner and exercises his office itself in a sinful way. This teaching in condemnation of that of the Donatists and Wycliff is well known. Viewed in the present context it is not surprising either. For the validity of a sacrament in the individual case is not identical with its fruitful reception. In the sacraments there can truly be a proffer of grace by God, actually promised by God on his part to men, and suspended over them in this period of the history of redemption as promise and summons, without by that very fact effecting their sanctification, by being applied and accepted and ratified by human freedom. Of course, this latter is again a grace of God, so that in the ultimate resort the institutional grace of the sacraments is not a matter of administration. The teaching concerning the baptism conferred by heretics is a classic example, especially as the "heretic" in the third century was always presumed to be culpably heterodox whether as dispenser or recipient of the sacrament.

The ultimate theological ground of this difference between validity and fruitfulness is on the one hand the circumstance that, in adults, grace as in fact effecting sanctification can only occur in a way that includes human freedom, while on the other hand this freedom itself must remain inaccessible to ultimate evaluation, before the coming of the judgment of God which alone will make all things known. The individual cannot promise himself from a sacrament the indefectible holiness of the Church as unambiguously his own; he must remain a pilgrim in fear and trembling leaving all to the judgment of God. This is precisely the reason why an actual official action of an individual minister cannot depend on his holiness, for otherwise the Church as represented in the acts of her minister would not be the invincible manifestation of redemptive grace, if such an act could be invalidated by the individual's guilt; or else the minister would know, as if by a sacrament that could not be without fruit, that he as an individual was justified by grace when he validly carried out an act of his office, and then he at least thanks to his office would have escaped from the condition of a pilgrim, not yet "justified" (1 Cor. 4:4).

But this distinction between possession of official authority and the holiness of ministry does not sufficiently describe the relation between office and grace. The fact is that the same relation holds here as in the question whether individual human beings who remain members of the Church can remain and be sinners, without detriment to the holiness of the Church. An affirmative answer must be given straightaway. But that does not mean that the personal holiness of her members is a matter of no importance to the Church's essence. The Church herself only exists by existing in her members. The holiness of "holy Church", which necessarily follows from the eschatological victory of grace, can therefore only consist in a personal holiness of her members. If all were sinners who had fallen away from the grace of God, holy Church herself would no longer exist. Despite the possibility, therefore, that individual human beings in the Church are sinners, and despite the fact that for that reason it remains uncertain in general until the death of the individual in which members of the Church of any age her holiness is realized, which members are in fact the bearers of the indefectible holiness of the Church, nevertheless God's will to bestow efficacious grace (the very will which gave the Church her being) rules over her, infallibly sanctifies her members, even if we do not know in detail which ones, and preserves them in grace, so that the Church never ceases to be holy. That same will must be operative too in regard to the Church's ministry if she is to be indefectibly holy and remain the presence and manifestation of the eschatologically victorious grace of Christ. A ministry impious throughout its exercise and a holy Church are incompatibles. If it were supposed that the ministry in its totality could accomplish its task without holiness, neither the holiness of the Church's members would essentially depend on the exercise of the ministry, which however it does, nor would the ministry remain what nevertheless it is, a ministry of sanctification for men.

THE VARIOUS SACRAMENTS

At first sight it might, of course, occur to someone to ask why the members of the Church should not receive from her ministers what the ministry can and is there to give them, and receive this *ex opere operato*, that is to say, independently of the holiness of the ministers dispensing the sacraments, and yet at the same time these ministers fail in their own lives to carry out in faith and love, what they do in their official capacity. The Church as a whole would still be a holy Church, even if she (or rather the one Church in so far as she was holy) consisted only of the "poor in spirit", the laity humbly receiving from the hierarchy. Let us leave out of account the fact that such a supposition imagines something impossible in real practice. For how could it be really possible for absolutely all bearers of office to reject the holiness which *ex supposito* is present in the Church, and which necessarily finds expression, is manifest, and consequently has a social and human and personal character and produces effects by inviting and convincing and bearing witness. Even apart from that, such a separation of office and holiness and its distribution between two subjects, is impossible. The ministry certainly has a power which is exercised *ex opere operato*. But if this *opus operatum* is in fact to be exercised in the Church (and it must be if the Church is to be and remain sanctified by the sacraments), God must not only ensure that if sacraments are administered, they are what they should be, but he must absolutely ensure that they are administered. God must will absolutely that in the Church (which is to be indefectible), the administration of the sacraments should take place. This, however, is inescapably and necessarily dependent on the subjective dispositions of men who administer them. In other words, the Church's rite must not only carry God's promise of inalienable validity if it is performed, because it is an

101

expression of the Church's inalienable validity as primal sacrament of grace, but God's formal and constitutive will must provide that the sacraments are actually administered, if the Church is to be what she is and if this essence of hers is to be actually realized. For not only the essence but also the existence of the Church are unconditionally willed by God. Consequently, if the sacraments belong to the Church's essence, the sacraments' actual existence in practice must be unconditionally willed by God.

But this existence of the sacraments does essentially depend on the holiness of those who dispense them. Of course, the individual minister can in fact carry out a sacramental rite in this or that instance without holiness, for alien motives, without its losing its essence or ceasing to exist. But that is impossible if applied to the whole of the Church's sacramental activity. It is not the efficacy of a sacrament actually administered that depends on its minister's being in a state of grace, but the perpetuation of sacraments in the Church as a whole and in the long run. If all the ministers were unbelieving and void of divine love and consequently if the gentle power were to disappear from the whole Church by which believing love induces even the faithless and the loveless in the Church to deeds which essentially really spring from faith and love (the administration of the sacraments is of that kind), could the administration of the sacraments itself survive in the long run? What reason would a body of ministers of that kind have still to remain true to their office? Is it thinkable that a reality should remain when its hold on existence has disappeared not only in this or that human being, but universally, as such? That would amount to explaining one and the same effect as capable of deriving from two disparate causes, which is impossible. So if God absolutely wills the existence of the sacraments in the whole Church, he must also absolutely will the holiness of the hierarchy as a whole, otherwise he would not will, what the actual factual existence of the administration of the sacraments depends on.

For the sake of closer consideration, it must be repeated that the typical instance of administration of the sacraments is not the baptism of infants, but the baptism of adults and the eucharist with an adult congregation. If anything of the kind is to take place, it can only be (looking at the totality of cases) when faith and receptiveness are found in the recipients. Otherwise there will be no one there to whom baptism can be administered or with whom the eucharist can be celebrated. The words of these sacraments can therefore only ever really be spoken in the context of the preaching of the faith. Those who have the power and authority to address God's sacramental words to men, have also the right and obligation to produce that context of affirmation of faith, in which alone these sacramental words *ex opere operato* encounter that disposition which is a situation within which the sacramental words can be uttered at all and heard with faith, and within which they have the power to produce their effect.[11] Now even though, once again, an individual instance of preaching of the faith is not dependent for its truth and claim on the faith of the hearers, simply on the faith and holiness of the individual who is preaching, nevertheless from the nature of the case, and according to the testimony of Scripture, testifying to the faith is in general essentially connected with the preacher's genuine

---

[11] From this it can be seen too that an absolute separation between power of order and power of jurisdiction, between *potestas ordinis* and *iurisdictionis*, is impossible in the Church.

witness in his own life, in other words, with his holiness. It has to be based on the "shewing of the Spirit and power" (1 Cor. 2:4) and a "spirit of power, of love and of sobriety" (2 Tim. 1:6–7). This proof of the inseparable connection between mission and authority to preach and personal and sanctifying charisma according to the testimony of Scripture, cannot be expounded in detail here.[12] Yet so that it is clear that this principle involves no element of Donatism, it should be noticed that every preacher of the faith bears witness, not to his own "private opinion", but to the belief of the Church. What he says, therefore, does not refer back to the fact that he, as a private person, is actually giving this testimony, but to the testimony of the Church as a whole. The Church, however, according to defined doctrine, is necessarily and indefectibly holy and as such is a motive of faith (Denzinger 1794). So what we have added to this teaching of the First Vatican Council in what we have been saying (which seems to us simply to expound what the Vatican Council taught), is only to say that it is not a merely factual relationship between the holiness of the Church and the motivation of faith, but an intrinsic and necessary one. The word of faith that calls for practical acceptance in faith and love, can only rightly be preached by the exercise of this faith and love, nor is it preached in any other way, for this is not possible in preaching that is done in the name of holy Church. Only in that way is such preaching really "witness", which is and must always be more than the communication of mere thought content. Consequently those who are entrusted with the power of the sacramental word are by the nature of the case (because this word can only be spoken in the context of the

---

[12] See K. Rahner, *Schriften zur Theologie* III (Einsiedeln ³1959) 306f.

words of faith as a whole), in principle also entrusted with giving testimony to the faith. But it is only really possible to bear witness to the faith by being a Christian oneself, that is, by one's own "holiness". For although the individual preacher by his preaching points to the holiness of the Church as a motive of faith and not merely or in the first place or expressly to his own, nevertheless this holiness of the Church is only present and existent in the holiness of individuals, the multitude in fact who actually form the Church which is holy. Such a necessary reference is consequently the affirmation that preaching is only testimony that calls for belief, when it is supported by the shewing of the Spirit; it implies, therefore, even when the individual preacher withdraws himself from the sanctifying power of the Spirit, the admission that the truth of Christ (which demands faith), must be proclaimed in holiness, even on the part of that individual preacher himself. For he cannot refuse as a demand on himself, what he needs to find actually realized in others, if his own preaching is to be possible, in others who are Christians and human beings just as he is. (It could be noted in addition here that someone who is publicly an unbeliever is thereby absolutely incapable of preaching in the name of the Church. Here again the final inseparability of office and life makes itself evident.)

Now this holiness, necessary and present in the whole and required of the individual, as testimony to the truth of the faith that is preached, is only possible through grace. The conferring by God of the office of administering the sacraments (which is only possible in the context of bearing witness to the faith), must therefore also necessarily imply the gift of grace, without which the carrying out of the functions of the office would be impossible. Otherwise God would be requiring something to be done, and at the same time making it impossible, by refusing the necessary means. Gift of ministry is therefore necessarily a proffer of grace to exercise the office. As, however, this conferring of ministry is, in fact, always a fundamental act of the indefectible Church and therefore is and remains a valid and true transmission of office, and can never be emptied of its significance and become outward show of such a transmission of power, the gift of grace on God's side in the rite of handing on of ministry is absolutely promised, it is *opus operatum,* a sacrament.

That in itself makes clear the ecclesiological aspect of the individual sanctification that occurs in the reception of holy order. The recipient of order receives his office as a grace, for he receives the grace which enables him to exercise his ministry as one that sanctifies him, and the grace to achieve the holiness that is essential to the really adequate fulfilment of his functions. Priestly holiness is not a question of a requirement that the priest should be a "pious man" in addition to carrying out the duties of his ministry, because after all, that is suitable and proper. The connection between office and priestly holiness is much closer and gives the latter itself an intrinsically ecclesiological aspect. The holiness of a priest is the living assimilation of his office, made possible by grace, and this assimilation in its turn, is a necessary factor in this office as a whole, in as much as this office includes the ministry of the word, as the setting and the exposition of the sacramental words.

For the working out on this basis of the idea of a priestly life and its essentially ecclesiological aspect, we must refer to our earlier treatment.[13]

[13] K. Rahner, *Schriften zur Theologie* III (Einsiedeln ³1959) 285–312.

7. Matrimony

Here too as with the discussion of holy order, a postponed question has to be answered: Why marriage is a sacrament, and how this can be shewn from the sources or from the more comprehensive principles of theology. St. Paul says explicitly (Eph. 5) that marriage is and should be in a certain way an image and an echo of the love between Christ and the Church. The double aspect of a reality which is both fact and exigence is found in all profoundly human things and need not arouse remark here. Yet to understand the statement is more difficult than is usually thought. Of course, with a little ingenuity anything can be compared with anything else. If conjugal unity and love only served in some such vague sense as a simile for the loving union between Christ and the Church, if the two realities were only being related metaphorically, the whole matter would be a very incidental one. That cannot be the intention.[14] Marriage and the covenant between God and humanity in Christ can not only be compared by us, they stand objectively in such a relation that matrimony objectively represents this love of God in Christ for the Church; the relation and the attitude of Christ to the Church is the model for the relation and attitude that belongs to marriage, and is mirrored by imitation in marriage, so that the latter is something contained or involved in the former. But why this is so, is not very easy to say. Of course, one can appeal to Paul's testimony, and this testimony of an apostle is indubitably fundamental. One can say that it is thereby

---

[14] The reader is referred to the more detailed interpretations of the text by biblical scholars, e. g. H. Schlier, *Der Brief an die Epheser* (Düsseldorf 1957) 252—280.

evidenced that God from the beginning in the garden of Eden created marriage to be such an image of the relation between Christ and the Church. But unless this symbolism is to be explained in a purely juridical and nominalist way, through the will of God viewed as quite extrinsic to the reality itself, and transcendent to it, and unless we are to rest content with the apostle's testimony as a mere matter of fact, without aiming at any understanding of the faith, we must certainly say that this will of God is operative in the reality itself, in marriage, and gives it a definite intrinsic characteristic which fits it for the function of symbol.

But then we must also say in what this characteristic consists. Only the answer to this question will furnish the reason why Paul knew what he tells us. Various factors might perhaps be suggested in explanation, though much more inquiry is called for, which cannot be undertaken here, for it would involve a consideration of practically the whole of revelation, as will be clear from the pointers which are all that are possible. A starting-point might be, that the different kinds of human love which give rise to genuinely human and personal relationship, are not only extrinsically comparable, but have a real interconnection as condition and foundation of one another. They are more than merely species of a merely logical genus, and conjugal love has a quite special place among them. Then, that being understood, one might indicate that Christ established the Church as the one "people of God", by entering the unity of "monogenetic" humanity (which is one through conjugal love) as a member of it. He loves men with a genuine love, and this, by accomplishing the sacrifice of the Cross, is of significance for the formation of the Church, while its power to establish a community rests on factors that concern the structure of the human condition generally and consequently stand in real relation to matrimony. The attempt might then be made to show that marriage has a real capacity to represent or typify God's love in Christ for the "one" humanity which he hallows by that love, and which we call the Church. This representative value is not a merely conceptual one formed in our minds, nor is it merely extrinsic, decreed by God.

Then one might delve deeper and show the very idea of man has its original, ultimate ground and basis in the idea of the God-man, and try to make it intelligible that the very possibility of man rests on the possibility (not the fact) of the God-man; that man is by origin what emerges not as a possibility, but as the possibility, when God as it were comes forth from himself into what is other than himself.[15] It would then have to be added that man, human being, means: "Male and female he created them." One would further have to add that Christ, by being envisaged from the beginning as the son born of woman, is willed formally and not merely *de facto* as a human being in a humanity of two sexes. One would have to say as well that the will to humanity (incarnation) itself necessarily, formally and implicitly involved the willing of the Church. If all these things (to which it is only possible to direct attention here), were thought out, it might perhaps be possible to grasp why authentic matrimony at all times has a truly representative value for God's unitive love in Christ for mankind.

If that were grasped, two further steps would have to be taken. It would have to be shown that this rôle of representation of Christians in the Church has to be carried out as a function

[15] See K. Rahner, *Schriften zur Theologie* IV (Einsiedeln 1960).

of the Church, because the Church in her members and through everything of which such members are capable, must show herself visibly and manifestly to be the beloved bride of Christ. That is, it would have to be shown that this representative function has to be exercised not only by Christians in as much as they are human beings, but in a higher degree through their being Christians and members of the Church. That would show that this typifying rôle, once Church and Christians exist, belongs within the Church as such. Then finally the second and last step could be taken. In fact it has been, by what has been said. Such symbolism of a fundamental kind, established in the very essence of the Church, is truly a fundamental act in which the Church fulfils her very nature, and consequently, in the Church, is a sign which produces what it signifies, and therefore, since it signifies grace, a sacrament. From that it would follow that it is the contracting of marriage which constitutes the sacrament of matrimony, and the reason for this would emerge. It is because this conjugal consent is itself one of the acts in which the Church's own nature is brought into activity, because in this consent of her members, she herself manifests herself as the mystery of the union between Christ and mankind.

This is also another of the cases in which, as in baptism by a layman in case of necessity (which in the light of the sacramental nature of baptism has nothing unusual or abnormal about it), not a cleric, but this or that Christian accomplishes an act of the Church herself, by "administering" the sacrament. Another example of that kind is seen in the sacrament of penance, where the acts of the penitent himself belong to the sacramental sign.[16]

[16] It is impossible here to investigate how it is possible for an unbaptized person validly to baptize and so accomplish an act of the Church.

With all these considerations in mind, the ecclesiological aspect of the sacrament of matrimony would then be clearly envisaged. For it would have emerged from these proofs of the sacramentality of marriage, that it is not only possible to compare marriage to the union between Christ and the Church, but that marriage itself contributes to it and indeed in a quite special way; and that the visible Church even in its historical reality appears as the bride of Christ, through her existence and characteristics bearing witness that in the Church, Christ has espoused humanity irrevocably to himself. In other words, it would have to be shown that marriage has a definite function in the Church, belongs to her full constitution and the full accomplishment of her nature, so that this is the objective reason for the sacramentality of marriage, the sacramentality of marriage being for us, once its existence is established, the means whereby this function in the Church can be recognized.

Finally, in this connection the following would need to be considered. We have already said how remarkable the relation between individual parish (local community) and the whole Church is. The local community is not only a member, a province of the whole Church. The whole Church is not only the sum of the parishes. Rather in the local church and its active accomplishment and self-realization, the whole Church in a true sense is manifested as a totality. What happens in the individual parish, especially in the celebration of the eucharist, renders unmistakably and really present, in its ground (the redemptive death of the Lord), the existence of the whole Church as the grace-giving presence of God. It testifies unambiguously to it and guarantees her nature and reality in the world. In view of this, and seeing that matrimony is an image of the alliance between Christ and the Church, we can say in a true sense of marriage that in it the Church is present; to the extent to which marriage realizes its own nature, as a valid marriage, sanctified by grace and lived in holiness. It is the smallest community but, for all that, a genuine community of the redeemed and sanctified, whose unity can build on the same foundation as that on which the Church is founded, the smallest of local churches, but a true one, the Church in miniature.

8. *The Anointing of the Sick*

The ecclesiological aspect of extreme unction, last anointing, cannot be indicated so readily. It is not easy here to get beyond the analogy of faith that suggests that if all the other sacraments have such an aspect, extreme unction cannot be lacking in this universal fundamental sacramental structure, either. Perhaps the following offers an approach. The nature of the Church is the starting-point. She is not an eternal welfare institute delivering, as it were, in the next world, to God, the successful results of her care for the salvation of souls, but with no inclination to see an end put to herself and her activity by the consummation of all things. She is rather the community of those who wait expectantly, looking with longing for the coming of the Lord and the approach of his final and perfect kingly rule. She is the Church who wills to be transformed into the eternal kingdom of God. Eschatological expectation is an essential component of the Church. But when does the Church actually exercise and practise it? In reply, it must be remembered that the Church is not a substance, but is realized in and through the individual human beings who are her members. They, however, are defined by their mortality. They are subject to death, and in it they experience an exceptionally distinctive situation of their eschatological expectation, hope and courage to transcend the world and the limits of their senses. The ineluctable situation of approaching death, with its accompanying distress, summons them practically compellingly to make up their mind about the ultimate meaning of their existence, in faith and hope and self-transcending love. This climax in the individual's eschatological position, being a concrete instance of eschatological hope, must also be an act in which the very nature of the Church is fulfilled. For the Church herself is the community of those who are on pilgrimage to the Lord in faith and love, and she only exists in individual human beings. And this is so not only because she endures in hope the mortal peril in her individual member (actual death need not necessarily supervene), but she herself must be able to stand by the sick person's bedside in her official and visible form. A Church incapable of doing so and who took her leave in embarrassment at the approach of death, as the "world" does, inevitably, because it has no hope, would not be the Church of eschatological hope, visibly and manifestly. Either that fundamentally eschatological attitude and activity would be lacking, or it would be unable to find expression when most called for, where the world really threatens to collapse, and the human being, and in him the actual Church in the concrete, are challenged whether they really dare audibly to speak words of Christian hope.

That does not quite bring us to the sacrament of extreme unction, but we have, nevertheless, reached the point where we can expect an act of the Church in the sick person and in his regard, that manifests the Church as overcoming death and its darkness by her eschatological hope. And in view of our general considerations so far, we can say that because such an act is a symbolic proclamation of the fundamental nature of the Church as instituted by Christ, the symbol is not empty, but renders present what it proclaims and therefore gives the saving grace of hope amid the ruin of death, which in this way becomes, instead of a death of Adam, the coming of Christ in the life of an individual. We have still not attained the sacrament of extreme unction, however, because, of course, it might be held that everything we are postulating could take place by the Church's giving the sick person that Body which, delivered to death, gives eternal life to those that receive it. Such a supposition would not be without foundation. We do pray *Esto nobis praegustatum mortis in examine.* And Jesus himself, as St. John shows, links the meaning of the eucharist very directly to the hope of resurrection and eternal life. The φάρμακον ἀθανασίας (medicine of immortality) has indeed a very great deal to do with that death in which true life comes to birth. And its reception is so much a sacrament of the dying that the Christian has a definite obligation to receive viaticum, which cannot be said to the same degree of extreme unction. All this, which is correct, should, however, not lead to the conclusion that the eucharist is the sacrament of the dying, since there must be one, and that there cannot be, and is not, any other.

For we observe that the various sacraments do not all stand in the same relation to each other, and that the degree of independence and distinct significance is not the same in each. Confirmation, for example, as we have already seen, is particularly connected with baptism and is in fact the completion of the rite of initiation, which fundamentally is already fully applied in baptism. And yet that does not disprove the existence of a separate sacrament which also has its meaning, for a part of the reality which was present in the other sacrament as *res sacramenti* is more clearly manifest as *sacramentum* in the new rite, which because it more distinctly represents this, also confers more deeply and abundantly what it represents. Similarly the Church herself calls anointing of the sick *consummativum* of the sacrament of penance (D 907). On this basis, then, we can now say without hesitation that it is quite possible and indeed to be expected that there is a rite which makes plain what is already fundamentally present in the eucharist as viaticum, and yet which is a separate sacrament. For since the eucharist is the daily bread of Christians, it cannot manifest so unmistakably a special symbolism celebrating eschatological expectation and firm hope of eternity, that it would be pointless for the Church and the individual close to death to testify to this hope specially, in a separate visible and tangible way. But if this happens, we have precisely the sacrament of extreme unction.

If what we have said is correct, (it has only been possible to indicate a line of thought), it will follow, conversely, that extreme unction has an ecclesiological aspect. For both in the sick person who, endowed with free will, (infants are not proper subjects of this sacrament), allows this anointing by a consent in faith, as a baptized member of the Church, and also in the Church's action, which bears witness that she is without despair at the approach of mortal agony for her member, and expresses her solidarity with him, the Church's nature is accomplished as the one who, when night falls on this world, raises the lamp of faith and goes to meet the bridegroom, daring to say, "Let grace come, and this world pass away. Maranatha" (*Didache* I, 6).

There are many other things which might be considered in regard to the theme dealt with in this essay. It would be possible, for example, to reflect how, as the liturgy demonstrates, the person administering a particular sacrament need not only be a physical individual, but can also be a group associated in unity. In this way it becomes clearer than ever that the Church herself fulfils her own nature when she acts in the individual. One might recall in this connection the imposition of hands of the *presbyterium* in ordinations, the concelebration of mass, the administration of extreme unction by several priests and the custom of the early Church in the sacrament of penance, of imposition of hands by the whole *presbyterium* in conjunction with the bishop.

One could recall too that not the whole life of the Christian although he is always and everywhere a member of the Church and exercises in everything a representative and sanctifying function for her, can be lived in the official and public domain of the Church as though it belonged to this and was a part of the formal accomplishment of the Church's nature in magisterium and sacraments and so on. But the existence of such a "private" Christian life in the members of the Church does not prevent there being an intrinsic similarity and a very close connection between their "private" Christian life *(in foro conscientiae)* and their official, public life in the celebration of the liturgy and reception of the sacraments. If in addition we remember that even in sacramental life the personal element is not replaced or really made easy or diminished, but, in adults, should find expression in the sacraments; and that a sacrament visibly manifests in time, within the Church, before her eyes and for the world, not only the action of God and of the Church, but also the interior act of the recipient's faith; it is clear that the sacraments contain implicit directions for the structure of the whole of Christian life even in its private domain. It would in fact be possible to sketch out a theology of Christian life in the concrete, on the basis of the sacraments. And since they all have an ecclesiological aspect, it would become clearer from it, that no one lives to himself; that each must bear another's burden; and that those who love their neighbour have fulfilled the law. Even in the most private sphere we are still one another's debtors. We are saved when we have forgotten ourselves on account of others. We are in blessedness when we have become those who, in the eternal kingdom of love, have found the Church of eternity, the beginning and promise of which is the Church who accomplishes her own life in the sacraments of Christ.

THE TRINITY
BY KARL RAHNER

Karl Rahner's emphasis in this book is on the central position of the doctrine of the Trinity. He shows that the God of the New Testament must be seen clearly as the free triune God, and that any tendency to unitarian monotheism endangers the vitality of the Christian message.

Karl Rahner faces up squarely to the odd situations in which, 'should the doctrine of the Trinity have to be dropped as false, the major part of religious literature could well remain virtually unchanged', for the Trinity is a reality that Christian piety generally has apparently decided to do without. With few exceptions theologians have shown little interest in the doctrine. Hence the Trinity has been present in recent theology, if at all, only in the vague sense of face-to-face contemplation of the triune God in the afterlife, and hardly as a reality that has much to do with us.

But Rahner asks how the contemplation of any reality, even the loftiest, beatifies us if intrinsically it is unrelated to us. He persuades us that we have to affirm an ontological connexion between the Trinity and man. As a profound mystery of salvation the Trinity affects us all closely.

In a brilliantly conceived and tautly composed sequence of essays, Karl Rahner amply substantiates his claim for the Trinity as a central doctrine of faith, and shows its indispensability for any logical theology of salvation. His is surely now the standard work on the Trinity, one of lasting importance.

ISBN 0 86012 015 5

THE HEART OF RAHNER
Edited by John Griffiths

An anthology of thoughts and meditations on central topics of the Christian life and faith, drawn from the theologian's most accessible works.

ISBN 0 86012 099 6

CHRISTIAN AT THE CROSSROADS
KARL RAHNER

In this important book for Christians living in an age of uncertainty, Karl Rahner speaks to the mood of the times. We are at the crossroads. We have to ask the really important questions: What is man? What is truth? What does being a Christian mean? What are prayer and penance? What is the right attitude to the enigma of death?

Karl Rahner offers a marvellously comforting message for all Christians. He reaches the heart of the average Christian, yet with an assurance of style and thought that never shirks the hard questions of the theologian. These are words of the spirit intended to point out not just one way ahead, but the right frame of mind and the right things to ask when choosing the way.

ISBN 0 86012 020 1

THE RELIGIOUS LIFE TODAY
KARL RAHNER

A sequel to *Christian at the Crossroads*. Karl Rahner examines the major issues which face the religious and indeed every conscientious Christian today. He searches relentlessly for the meaning of essential Christianity, starting with the Christian message as offered to and received by men and women at the present time, and then examining its significance in the religious life.

This is a stirring, hopeful and eminently sensible book for all Christians: 'Christianity is hope,' he writes. 'Christianity is love of one's neighbour, and a love of one's neighbour which draws its ultimate strength from a liberating contemplation of the crucified and risen Jesus. . . . The more we are who we want and ought to be, the more grows the chance, the prospect, the hope that our religious life in the Church will continue not just to hold its ground, not just to survive, but to serve God, men, and thereby also the Church.'

ISBN 0 86012 028 7

ENCYLOPEDIA OF THEOLOGY
EDITED BY KARL RAHNER

A Concise Sacramemtum Mundi

The *Encyclopedia of Theology* offers more than 1800 pages of thought and information on the major themes of traditional and modern theology. Its aim is to provide a basic text presenting the findings of modern scholarly thought and research into the main themes of the theological disciplines. It draws on the work of an international team of 600 theologians, exegetes and specialists in various fields, and contains major articles dependent on contributions by more than 200 experts in the natural and human sciences.

The *Encyclopedia of Theology* is open in spirit and approach. It is an essential and reliable reference work and manual of the Christian faith for individual or group use and contains hundreds of articles on topics from Ethics to Resurrection, Language to Protestantism, Atheism to the Trinity. No responsible and inquiring Christian can afford to be without it.

'The publication of this encyclopedia is a reminder of what riches the rest of us are gaining as, more and more, the separations of Christians are being overcome . . . on their side these Roman Catholic theologians are thoroughly ecumenical in temper . . . This encyclopedia is a convincing, because never polemical, proof of a theological renewal . . . it is (its) achievement to indicate an approach which Protestants and Catholics can take together into the truth and into the future.'
— *Church Times*

'In this encyclopedia the interested reader will find much that is valuable, thoughtful and stimulating for further thought and study . . . it is difficult if not impossible to recommend any comparable single-volume work for English language readers.'
— *The Furrow*

'A modestly priced theological library.'
— *The Tablet*

'A book which can be recommended with great conviction.'
— *Catholic Herald*

ISBN 0 86012 006 6

CONCISE THEOLOGICAL DICTIONARY
BY KARL RAHNER AND HERBERT VORGRIMLER
Second Edition

The *Concise Theological Dictionary* was written to provide explanations of the most important concepts of Christian theology. It was first published in Germany in 1961 and in Great Britain four years later. Now the dictionary, for its second English edition, has been thoroughly revised and augmented, based on the tenth German edition. The articles have been revised, many have been substantially or entirely rewritten, and a number of new articles have been added. The result is a definitive text for the modern age.

All this new work makes the second edition of the *Concise Theological Dictionary* also a courageously forward-looking yet orthodox compendium of Christian teaching which incorporates the evolution of theological thought and scholarship as well as ecclesiastical deliberations from Vatican II onwards. 'Theology in the last quarter of this century,' the authors write, 'has to answer more attentively to criticism than when the first edition of this book was conceived. We have tried to confront several new aspects of theology, but without seeming to claim that Christianity knows the answer to everything.'

ISBN 86012 108 9

KARL RAHNER: AN INTRODUCTION TO HIS THEOLOGY
By Karl-Heinz Weger

A survey of the main themes that recur in Rahner's writings. Karl Rahner himself praised this book as the best existing introduction to his work.

ISBN 0 86012 094 5

THE COURAGE TO PRAY
BY KARL RAHNER AND J.B. METZ

With his ability to shed unexpected light on traditional themes, Karl Rahner explores the age-old practice of prayer to the saints. Johann Metz develops aspects of prayer associated with the political theology for which he is famous. The two theologians show that there is no substitute for prayer, which is a basic human impulse and necessity. Christians, however strong their conviction, need the courage to pray in the face of the indifference and trials of modern life. This book offers such encouragement to personal prayer.

ISBN 0 86012 107 0

OUR CHRISTIAN FAITH
BY KARL RAHNER AND KARL-HEINZ WEGER

Two leading Catholic theologians offer a thought-provoking exchange of ideas on the essence of Christian faith. Above all they try to answer the question: Can we live the Christian faith today with conviction and intellectual honesty? They examine the main tenets of Christian belief as they affect men and women in contemporary life, and never evade the difficult points but examine them with care for truth.

ISBN 0 86012 108 9

Books of general Christian interest as well as books on theology, scripture, spirituality and mysticism are available from the publishers Burns and Oates and Search Press Limited. A catalogue will be sent free on request.

Burns and Oates
Search Press Limited
Wellwood, North Farm Road, Tunbridge Wells, Kent TN2 3DR
Tel. (0892) 44037/8